ENOUGH BALLS TO FINISH

GOLF'S LESSONS ON RETIRING WELL

GEORGE K SLYMAN JR.

DAVID,
KEEP 'EM IN
THE SHORT
GRASS.

Outskirts Press, Inc.
Denver, Colorado

The opinions expressed in this manuscript are solely the opinions of the author and do not represent the opinions or thoughts of the publisher.

Enough Balls to Finish
Golf's Lessons on Retiring Well
All Rights Reserved
Copyright © 2007 George K Slyman Jr
V2.0

Outskirts Press
http://www.outskirtspress.com

ISBN-13: 978-1-4327-0337-0

Outskirts Press and the "OP" logo are trademarks belonging to
Outskirts Press, Inc.

Printed in the United States of America

CONTENTS

INTRODUCTION

"Ultimately, what I want to be able to do as I approach the latter stages of my life is to look at all that has happened to me as one eighteen hole round."
– Greg Norman (T&L Golf, Jan/Feb '05)

Golf and retirement are both aspirational pursuits.

The road to retirement, in whatever form that takes for you, is very much like a full round of golf. Our front nine is full of youthful optimism and anticipation. The round holds great promise in its early stages. Enthusiasm seems tied to the quality of those early shots. Great shots lift us and increase the promise of a score that will be worth the effort. On the other hand, poor shots can take the wind from our sails and leave us wishing we hadn't begun. A full round is nothing short of an exercise in patience.

The deeper we get into our round the more we realize the significance of every shot. Some might like to throw away the scorecard midway through, but life's format is stroke play where every shot or attempt counts, for better or worse. Seldom are we granted a mulligan and we must carry the weight of a poorly struck shot all the way to its conclusion.

This book is about the parallels of the game of golf and our financial round of life. It is about the lessons we can take from golf and apply them to our march towards retirement, and the intellectual honesty and accountability that will be required of us along the way. Those we play with, the equipment we carry with us and how we think, all affect the outcome of our round.

You can be excessively innovative or strive for simplification. No matter how you play or where you are in your round so far, you can learn a little in the pages that follow.

REWARD &
JUSTICE

"Most of us don't really know how well we're doing, in real life, and imagine we're doing not so bad. The world conspires to flatter us; only golf trusts us with a cruelly honest report on our performance."
- John Updike, Learning the Game

Those of us who know and love golf understand the manifold reasons we play. To many of the 'great unwashed' golf is a non sequitur. In their opinion it takes too much time, causes too much frustration and requires too much precision to be enjoyable. Those reasons, for the golf enthusiast, are a bit too anemic to keep us off the course. It is a wonderfully intoxicating pursuit with a mercurial quality that taunts you to come back one more time and get it right.

The golf course itself is part of the reason we play. It is a verdant, lush open piece of land that offers a sense of expansive freedom. Very often golf courses look as though they've been there from creation, fitting in with the landscape so naturally that you couldn't imagine their absence. There is a sense of both expectation and calm before a round, anticipation for the challenge and appreciation for the beauty of the surroundings. The uncomfortable notion of a poorly played round is balanced by the knowledge that at the very worst you've paid for a great view.

There is freedom in golf, freedom to walk or to ride, freedom to choose your own weapon, freedom to not return phone calls, and freedom to know that for the next few hours you will escape the world's pace and pressure and spend time in the company of some carefully chosen friends.

There is also accountability in golf. The accountability to know and accurately report your score, to ascertain what types of trouble may lie ahead of you, to have some inclination of your ability in given circumstances, and to respect the social aspects of your interactions with those in your group. It is this part of golf that changes the outcome and enjoyment factor of each round. Granted, a slight change in pin placement or tee box distance changes the dynamic slightly, but the personal aspects of golf paint a different picture on an otherwise continuous canvas.

Anyone who ever had an Etch-a-Sketch knows what I mean. At the end of a round, if the results were not in keeping with expectations we can turn it upside down, give it a shake, erase the recent past and begin anew.

Golf gives us a fresh canvas to work with for each outing, and the image we record is ours alone.

Golf, more than most team sports today, appears to be a reflection of a truth in our society that too many are unwilling to admit. It is an individual game where no blame can be laid at the feet of another. We cannot claim that someone dropped our pass. We cannot say that we didn't get enough playing time. Although our focus and attention may ebb and flow during our round, we play every minute of our own game. In a society that is quick to point the finger of blame and liability, golf stands out as an endeavor that has an wholeness in its solitude. It requires honesty and accountability which is what our own lives also require of us. Try finding that in large supply today.

You may not have noticed, and you may not be alone, but if you've finished your formal education and started full time employment, *you're already off the first tee.* This is the way most people enter their round… unaware, unprepared and unadvised, hacking their way from one hazard to another without any forethought. You will be happy to know it is never too late to check the condition of your equipment, check the wind direction and look for the hazards even if you think you have already entered your 'back nine.'
You will need to understand three fundamental things:

- What is your par?
- How is this course laid out?
- Where is the trouble?

THE GREAT EQUALIZER

"One man's ceiling is another man's floor."
- Paul Simon

Minot, North Dakota. It had the distinction of being the most affordable housing market a couple of years ago, according to Coldwell Banker Home Price Comparison Index. You can get a 2,200 square foot home for about $130,300. You could get the equivalent home in La Jolla, California for about $1,708,300. That's thirteen times the price… If that's too much for you to tackle all at once, how about a little leverage? With a thirty year mortgage the extra monthly payment is a manageable $10,438 per month.

Before you dismiss either location remember there are a lot of similarities to consider. The houses are the same size, there's a nice roof over your head in bad weather, there is a hospital nearby, and you can get satellite television in either location. The population in each city is about 40,000 give or take a little. At least one of the local public golf courses has 18 holes, carts and sandwiches. Green fees differ a bit. Torrey Pines will run 'out-of-towners' $150 on the weekend, while Souris Valley will set you back $16.

So then, what gives with the big disparity in price? It might be a little thing we call the 'desirability factor.' But who decides that La Jolla is so desirable? A lot of people I suppose, but not necessarily you. Desirability drives what you want and when you want it. Desire is a dangerous word. It can tilt the balance between 'eat well and sleep well.' It can point you in the direction of a lifestyle, but create its own stumbling block along the way to its achievement.

You must determine what it is you want out of your retirement, and just how badly you want it. There is bound to be a collision some day. It will be between your vision of retirement and what reality has in store for you. A lot of what you do today determines what your life will look like during those last twenty, thirty or more years.

Nothing against Minot. Their golf season is a bit shorter and they're using shovels for a few months while people in La Jolla are using nine-irons. Although I've never been there, I suspect the drivers may honk their horns a lot less than people in Southern California. In La Jolla, I also came across what had to be the best dressed pan handler in America. He was clean cut with designer jeans, Airwalk shoes, Maui Jim shades and a Starbucks mug extended arrogantly to those passing by. He looked more like a grad student trying to pay off student loans. Maybe Minot has legitimate pan handlers, or at least grad students with a work ethic. But I stray from my point.

Unfortunately for some, retirement might consist of sitting on the front porch counting the passing cars. For others it may involve a pause from work to enjoy some travel, some lessons to bring down the handicap before returning to the same or a new occupation. Will you be playing the local municipal course for twelve dollars, and be happy? What will your view be like? Will you have to grind it out because your surroundings didn't end up as picturesque as you would have hoped? Will you take satisfaction in the freedom you have or will the frustration of your performance keep you from any sense of fulfillment at all?

That's the way it is

Walter Cronkite was once asked how his retirement was going, he reportedly answered, "It sucks." I doubt that Walter was running low on cash. I would suspect that his comment had to do with his mental adjustment. Well, Walter, that's the way it is.

The way Americans work, play, live and 'retire' has changed over the last 30 years, and is changing still. In fact, the concept of retirement slipped into the American lexicon probably about 1935. Social Security arrived on the scene then and it gave all classes of society a mile marker of age and a floor for 'unplugging' which they had not previously had. Until that time you could not consider doing nothing until you could absolutely afford to do nothing, and few fit into that category. At the time Social Security was introduced, its purpose was partially to help those ravaged by the Great Depression, and partially to address the 25% unemployment rate by inducing some older workers to come off of the payrolls and make room for younger labor.

Webster's dictionary defines *"retirement"* as 'withdrawing from action, withdrawing for privacy, or withdrawing from one's occupation.' Throughout America's history we've never really been a people known to withdraw. That seemed a more natural inclination of the French. Sorry, couldn't resist.

Enjoyment is more our style. Perhaps 'excessive' enjoyment might categorize us best, or at least the appearance of enjoyment. That is due in large part to the fact that we squeeze our enjoyment in to smaller slices of time than most other countries. Our work hours are traditionally longer than other western countries. We have fewer holidays as well. So the typical harried American tries to shoehorn three weeks of activity into one week's vacation. The truth is we're not very good at extended periods of leisure time. We succumb to guilt if we are apart from our responsibilities for too long. We question whether we deserve the time or if it might be too much of an indulgence to have this much fun.

Do you remember the beer commercial that said, 'You only go around once in life, grab all the gusto you can.' They were right, except I don't think beer was the answer. As most people believe, we only get one shot at this life. Of course there are different schools of thought, such as my cousin Tom, who thought he wouldn't live beyond age fifteen and then eventually come back as a Coke bottle. It is amazing that people who start off like that can actually end up living normal lives. At any rate, we really should grab as much as we can, 'gusto' being open to interpretation.

Sometimes we push at the pace of a sprint when we should be pacing ourselves for a marathon. There have been so many analogies using the marathon but the only one that makes sense at all was the original account. The Greek soldier Pheidippides had run 26 miles from the town of Marathon to the city of Athens to deliver a message. He arrived with enough strength to say "Niki!", or 'victory.' He then fell to the ground and died. This occurrence seemed like such a great idea to emulate that today thousands around the world strap on the sneakers to run 26 miles, delivering absolutely no message at all. Ask one of them who crosses the finish line, 'What have you come all this way to tell me?' Nothing. I figure if you're going to engage in something that grueling, make sure it's got a purpose or a message at its end. Pace yourself.

Some get the sense during retirement of being at a snail's pace while the world zips by, and it eventually lures a good many back into a quicker pace. If you've ever had the experience of being in a foursome that was playing so slow and were asked multiple times whether someone behind could play through, you know what I mean. Even the marshal can take you out of rhythm just by his presence. You are aware that you should be moving along because someone, somewhere told you this round should be played in 4 hours 20 minutes. Undoubtedly, courses have business profits to consider, but do you suppose Old Tom Morris was troubled by such time constraints? His biggest nuisance was a herd of grazing sheep.

By most accounts the Scots get the credit for the origins of golf. This is a gift to the world surpassed only by the gift of the musical platypus, those beautiful bagpipes. I believe providence most mercifully had a hand in the broad acceptance of one over the other. By loose accounts, the game derived its name from the initial rules it invoked, which would explain my wife's lack of affinity for the four letter game. Men's clubs had signs that read 'Gentleman Only, Ladies Forbidden,' and so the world's finest acronym was born.

The Dutch probably take issue with those accounts considering they claim they played a game called 'kolf' back in the 1400's. Whatever its origin, it has undoubtedly changed quite a bit throughout history. The wild rolling unmanicured hills with rabbit holes as the ultimate target, and sticks hewn from branches to move along a rock eventually gave way to precision instruments, carpet-like fairways and composites from the table of elements in both club and ball construction.

Retirement, as we think about it now, is a relatively recent development and as we look back over its short history we can see the rapid evolution of its place in our lives.

At the turn of the 20th century the pattern of life had been:

•Birth... Work... Death.

Then an educational revolution began and the pattern became:

•Birth... Education... Work... Death.

Then entered the concept of 'retirement' and 'leisure' time.

Lifecycle

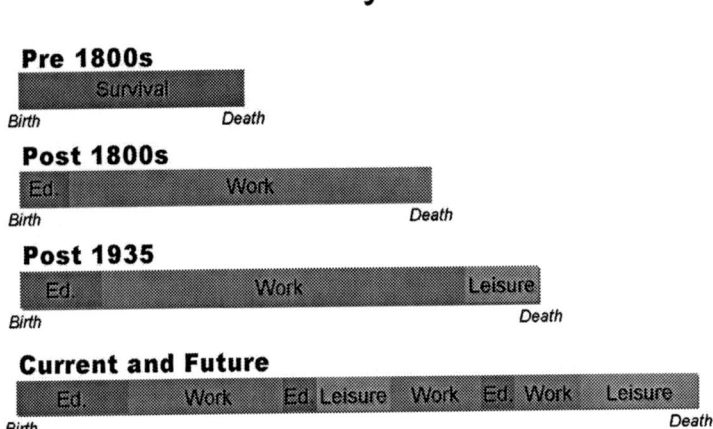

Pre 1800s
Survival
Birth   Death

Post 1800s
Ed.   Work
Birth   Death

Post 1935
Ed.   Work   Leisure
Birth   Death

Current and Future
Ed.   Work   Ed. Leisure   Work   Ed. Work   Leisure
Birth   Death

In fact, golf began to really take off as leisure time

became a status symbol. It was the social class with the availability of leisure time that primarily engaged in the sport. Just as our economy soared in the late 1990's so did the number of rounds played and the number of new golfers entering the sport. The skid of 2000-2002 impacted the golf industry in a way that it is still recovering from. Attempts by industry analysts to reignite interest in golf are primarily focused on the issue of time. The most common complaint recreational golfers have about not being able to get out enough is the lack of time. The round takes too much time. With family activities filling the schedule an large demographic of participants have cut back. Family friendly tee times, shorter rounds, unconventional 6 and 9 hole executive rounds and family activities are ways in which they seek to lure the golfer back.

Leisure time has become more structured, more subject to the calendar and far less spontaneous than it once was. Retirement is starting to take on that structure as well. It just may be that the new concept for retirement will not involve 'withdrawal' at all but rather a series of mini-careers following an initial career, each with its own set of educational requirements and newly acquired skills. Whatever it looks like for you is a personal matter, and the clearer and earlier your vision, the better off you will be.

THE LUXURY INFERNO

"Golf is the equivalent of crack for middle-aged white men."
- *Mike Barnicle, journalist/talk radio host*

I've noticed over the years that the real money is made by those who fan the flames of desire, those who paint the vivid pictures of what style and success look like and then try to sell it to you in a package that usually requires some level of financing. If that is the case, then we are witnessing the five alarm inferno in both the luxury and 'wanna-be' markets. Indulgence and the need to demonstrate (or feign) status are at all all-time high and expected to grow considerably in the next decade.

According to the USA TODAY, Wal-Mart's sales were only up 3% in 2004; Neiman Marcus' were up 11%. As a nation we spent $50 billion on food, coffee and wine, fully half the amount that we spent on new homes and home renovations. The food is more often of the specialty nature, the coffee comes in $4.75 cups of Venetian Tahitian Venti. Wine, with its consumerism trending as it has from white Zinfandel to Cabernet to Shiraz, doesn't taste quite as full bodied if it wasn't first spotted in a full page color ad in a gourmet magazine. We've watched as entry level BMW's, Jaguars, and Mercedes, and lower cost silver jewelry from Tiffany's bring a demographic group into a market they previously felt was unattainable. We have all heard that a luxury once enjoyed, becomes a necessity, and some are seeing to it that remains the case.

Consumerism gets bigger and more onerous every day. Luxury purchases are at an all-time high and the pace of the growth in the luxury market is twice that of the retail market. Although there does seem to be a shift in what type of luxury things we buy.

Bon Appetit Magazine holds an annual celebrity chef golf weekend where they extract hundreds of dollars from those desperate enough to want to out-drive a crepes flipper in a floppy hat. Yes, culinary lovers, it is true, you can play 18 holes with a celebrity chef. (In their defense the money goes to some presumably worthwhile charity.) Could you imagine the utter outrage and horror of ordering a chili dog at the turn with that crowd? You will cement your place in the culinary world as the 'barbarian with a pedestrian taste'. Better that, I suppose, than a cart girl demanding that you choose between a pan seared and deglazed foie gras or baby calves liver sautéed in apples. I'll take the tuna on rye with a light beer, thanks.

The marketing drive toward luxury is directed at the boomer generation who, according to many studies, is the demographic least likely to give up their level of lifestyle, wants and desires as they move into retirement. The apple has not fallen far from the tree as members of the middle section of the Boomer Nation are beginning a trend similar to their parents' snow-bird migration. It is called splitting and involves owning properties elsewhere that are used about five times per year for three or more days. Fractional ownership is part of that trend. All this while still fully employed. It is all a product of leveraging increased income and higher debt ratios.

Contrast that with the previous generation who may have coined the phrase 'cut back'. I suspect that a great deal of this mentality among the boomers is fed by the notion that they will inherit their parents' wealth. According to the demographic studies, trillions of dollars are estimated to change hands from one generation to the next. Somehow I don't think the increasing expense of long term health care was factored in to that calculation, and I suspect the net transfer will be far smaller than expected. Nevertheless, the boomers are at the front of the indulgence curve.

There has been somewhat of a shift to luxury services and experiences from the items themselves. Spas are popping up everywhere. More and more courses are now referring to themselves as 'such-and-such Golf Course and Spa'. If your local municipal course sticks a hot tub out behind the pull carts you can expect the fees to go up commensurately. Is it possible that the greens keeper you once knew as Pete, will now be referring to himself as Sven, and tempting you with some scented oils and a Swedish massage? Make sure he washes his hands first.

The change has come about in parallel over the last two decades in both the financial marketplace and the recreational marketplace. I hesitate to draw an absolutely direct connection between golf and economic prosperity, but the evidence is there. There are now about as many public play golf courses as there are mutual funds (12,000+) both increasing dramatically since 1990. Funds have sprung up with increasing specialty – Sector, Niche, Emerging Markets, Hedge, Rotation, and the like. The golf courses have increased mostly in the 'upscale daily fee' category. Those courses compete with, and have directly cut into the desirability of the private country club category. In fact, the number of private clubs has declined over the last fifteen years as competition in high-end public courses has increased. Older private clubs struggle to keep up with the appetite for variety in course play and the services and amenities provided. Upscale daily fee courses have tested the thresholds of their price breaks and found that more people will part with $250 to play a round on a resort course, than will part with the fifteen to twenty thousand dollars for initiation fees at a private course. It follows the luxury car lease-versus-buy argument. The old status quo of

Friday night cocktail socials as a lure, is fading. Swimming pools, massage services, family oriented layouts are often too appealing to ignore. Not to mention the far more sophisticated public relations spin by new clubs to create buzz and desirability, giving the new courses the 'place to play' status.

The pace of play in the luxury world is fast. High end courses will have to be innovative to keep up. The price expected for the 'exclusivity' of a private club is getting harder and harder to work into a balanced equation given some of the alternatives. It will likely take more than a cold wash cloth and a Hummer-style beverage cart to meet growing expectations.

ACCESSIBILITY

"Although golf was originally restricted to wealthy,
overweight Protestants, today it's open to anybody
who owns hideous clothing."
- Dave Barry

Other factors often overlooked are the demographic changes taking place in both the golf world and the financial world. Golf in the United States is no longer the exclusive domain of wealthier old men. Or white men. It has taken on a palette of colors, thanks in large part to a young Afro-Asian California man. Women have represented the largest demographic increase in rounds played in the last decade. Michelle Wie is probably going to magnify that greatly in the next ten years.

Now consider the world of investing. Most of you can remember Sir John Houseman telling us that at Smith Barney, "We make money the old fashioned way. We earrrrn it." The old school brokerage houses have taken a beating by some of the newer quicker internet based clearing houses like E*Trade, TD Ameritrade and Scottrade. Ever increasing menus of features and customization made the trading broker, sitting at his desk, a dinosaur. He no longer had the exclusive access to information because it was everywhere. **He had to compete on interpretation** and that presumes you know something that others don't.

The margins of profitability in the old brokerage houses dropped like rocks and newer strategies became necessary. As dual income households became more the norm the retirement account was not just in Ozzie's name but in Harriett's as well. All the while the number of mutual funds tripled during the 1990's making caution and analysis that much more imperative.

Do you recall the phrase 'membership has its privileges' from the American Express Card? Visa crushed their perception of exclusivity by touting *access* as the privilege to strive for. More availability. Younger investors who jumped on the 401k and internet bandwagons changed the landscape of buying and selling stocks. Technology made the access and delivery of information radically different. The shifting landscape of online brokerage mergers and acquisitions will make the consistency of information a key variable.

Demand for more pushes the envelope. In excess of 200 channels on satellite and cable TV, unsolicited emails, pop-up ads and free magazine subscriptions keep us wondering what's out there and what's available. Now the noise for your attention, the 'buzz' telling you what you've got to have, is so loud it affects not only how we prepare for our vision of retirement, but tests us whether we can remain focused and prepare at all.

ANTICIPATION

*"Conscience, in most men, is but the anticipation of
the opinions of others."*
- Sir Henry Taylor

Does information change our behavior? There is no
question that we live in a state of anticipation which is
governed by the information sources we rely on.
Consider the Weather Channel or even your local
channel's forecast. If a heat wave is predicted,
businesses prepare their employees to stay home and
telecommute, there is an early run on air conditioners
and fans, and tee times are cancelled. It's as though
summer caught everyone by surprise and the five day
outlook is the only thing that caused us to know what
season we are in.

The effects of widely broadcast information can
obviously cost a number of industries a lot of
business. Not long ago a large group of golf course
owners proposed to sue the Weather Channel for its
acknowledged bias toward the pessimistic. If there
were a chance of rain in the vicinity during the day,
they would post 'showers likely.' That inclination
toward pessimism kept people off of golf courses,
away from beaches and amusement parks.

Twenty-five years ago people would wake up, go to
work, and if conditions were bad enough, they would
go home. Now we live in anticipation. (The flip side

of that is the bonus that ski resorts get from the anticipation of a storm, even if it fizzles out. Fool me once, ski on grass. Fool me twice, sit on my ...couch.)

CADDIES, CART PARTNERS & CLAIRVOYANTS

"If your caddie coaches you on the tee, 'Hit it down the left side with a little draw,' ignore him. All you do on the tee is try not to hit the caddie."
- Jim Murray

CADDIES

Golfer (screaming): "You've got to be the worst caddy in the world!"

Caddy: "I doubt it. That would be too much of a coincidence!"

Tom Watson will tell you how important Bruce Edwards was to him. Phil Mickelson will probably say the same about Bones. The relationship between player and caddie can make, break or complicate a career, a tournament or a round. Come to think of it, Ian Woosnam and his uncounted 15th club may also have an opinion. It is a trust relationship which when it is at its best, becomes synergistic. If your career depends to any degree on someone, that person should be chosen carefully. It also is going to cost you something. Most professional caddies on tour have a tiered income system. Five percent of earnings if their player makes the cut and is in the money, seven percent if he's in the top ten, and ten percent if he wins. I call that having a vested interest in your player's performance.

If you've never played with the services of a caddie, it's important to know that the ground rules are the key. Before a round you need to set the expectations. What do you want from your caddie? Ask for, or expect too much and you'll be disappointed. " I need you to point out the hazards that aren't plainly obvious...I need you to tell me what my yardage is and I'll pick the club...Don't leave my equipment unattended...Keep my conditions as favorable as possible by cleaning my grips and my clubfaces...Try to keep an eye on my ball when I hit it"...etc. Notice that I haven't expected my caddie to lower my score, increase my talent or erase my own spastic blunders. He just hands me the club, I've got to hit it. Now we're on the same page. If he's been at it long enough I might ask for his past experience on a testy green, but I've got to hit the line and make my putts. I would also expect him to have a good basic knowledge of the rules of golf to keep me from being penalized unnecessarily.

Imagine this. You have a lesson scheduled with a local pro. You arrive early and you are milling around the pro shop. He sees you looking at a training device from one of those television infomercials. Sensing your interest he tries to sell you the new device before your lesson. It may be a great teaching tool and have worked wonders for countless others, but you are unique. Think about it – he knows nothing about your game, your tendencies or your faults. He is trying to give you a solution before he knows if there is a problem.

I had a prospective client come in after visiting a few other planners. He told me that a local planner at his first introductory appointment told him that he needed a Rabbi Trust. Was he running a special that day? What's next, scheduling the traveling moile for a middle aged briss? In thirty minutes he concluded that this person needed additional layers of complexity. Prescription without diagnosis. It was a boastful attempt by the planner to flaunt expertise. Of course there is the occasion when you've danced all over your financial bunker and the burden of raking up your mess is daunting. But that requires cleaning up and simplifying, not adding more layers of 'stuff.'

Watch for anyone attempting to complicate your financial life. There is a simplicity that lies beyond sophistication.

That being said, simplification does not mean

simplistic. Your advisors should have an ample supply of intelligence. Try not hiring someone whose IQ falls somewhere between a boarder collie and a baked potato.

CART PARTNERS

"To be stupid, selfish, and have good health are three
requirements for happiness, though if stupidity is
lacking, all is lost."
– Gustave Flaubert

Newport California is a beautiful area. It has some wonderfully challenging and scenic golf courses. On a recent business trip we called ten days in advance to schedule the earliest possible tee time at Pelican Hill's South course. (It never hurts being on east coast time.) My golfing buddy and I enjoyed our round and the company of two gentlemen who joined us. One of them had played there before and gave us an occasional heads-up on difficult carries and hidden bunkers. As a foursome we helped one another by finding distance markers, keeping an eye on errant shots and the like. You know, the typical courteous golf experience. They were all patient when I pulled out my camera to take a few pictures. It was a completely enjoyable round.

In all relationships, regardless of the duration, there is a factor that can push you over the edge, though...I refer to the experience of the *bad cart partner*.

A couple of days after the Pelican Hill experience we headed over to Strawberry Farms which is a nice course (back nine being far more scenic that the front, by the way.) Once again we were paired with two unknowns, except this time we took the opportunity to each ride with one of our new acquaintances. It took about two holes for my cart partner to show his true colors. With him behind the wheel we drove consistently to his ball first, even if he was further down the fairway. The discussion down the cart path was about his next shot, his club selection, what went wrong and his score. He never asked if I had the clubs I needed or if I wanted him to wait for me. He expected the rest of the foursome to have some idea of where his ball had gone, but never offered any suggestion of anyone else's direction. It was, in summary, an invitation to bury one of my irons in his forehead and cover him in a shallow bunker. For the record, let's call him Chris, because that was his real name. Defamation laws prevent me from giving you his last name. The contrast was vivid from my previous round and my enjoyment level was distinctly different. Even in this beautiful God-given game of golf, there are times when eighteen holes can seem like a week with your mother-in-law.

If your advisor is all about him - leave, and do it quickly. He should be asking about you, your current circumstances, your vision of your future, your previous experiences both good and bad. If he's going to be your financial cart partner he should be exploring as much as possible about *your* taxes, *your* current holdings and debts, *your* expenses and *your* perceived obligations to others. That last point is important and almost always overlooked. Our perceptions drive our actions. If you're an only child and expect that you alone will be responsible for caring for your elderly parents, an advisor needs to know that. If you believe it will be your obligation to finance your grandchildren's college education, then that will impact how much you save and how aggressively you invest a portion of your funds. None of that will be explored if Chris is driving your financial cart.

Cart Partner- the good. Sometimes a good cart partner helps your game. He or she can be a great asset to your focus and the ease with which you complete a round. He helps you locate your shot, takes you to your ball, brings your putter if you've forgotten it. He's not just looking out for himself. Ask him this: How many potential clients have you turned away over the last year? Then ask yourself the following: Would you take on a relationship that is not a good fit? He shouldn't either, and if he's got enough experience under his belt he should have started occasionally turning away business for that very reason.

Find a good cart partner, whether it's an attorney, accountant or financial advisor. Don't try to go the distance with someone who is not a good fit. It'll be costly, especially deep into your round.

CLAIRVOYANTS

*"It is very hard to predict, especially about the
future."*
- Niels Bohr

I sometimes joke with my clients that the letters after my name stand for Clairvoyant Financial Prognosticator. Far too often an advisor will almost intimate knowledge of the future. He gives the impression he can surmise when the market is going up and for how long. He may tell you that double digit returns this year are practically a given. He will use past performance of a fund as road map for the future with little margin built in for error. Try adding the opinions of an economist to that mix it will cloud the issue even further. In fact, it's been said that if you get five economists in a room you'll get six different opinions.

Often the worst advice you can get is the type that has no accountability attached to it. It happens at cocktail parties, business meetings, on golf courses and other social settings. It is the persuasive argument made for a fund, a stock, or some rumor of impending action at a company and usually has, at its root, a desire on the part of the persuader for the higher standing. Perhaps they want to be viewed as knowledgeable in front of their peers. Similar drivel can be found on countless internet blogs offered up by disembodied pseudo experts.

You can count on this general rule:
Peoples' opinions move in the direction of the greatest conviction.

Most people infer a sense of certainty from conviction and that is a horrible error. **Conviction can be very genuine and absolutely wrong at the same time.**

Finances have always been a topic of social conversation. Golf can certainly be a social game. Although many of us enjoy a round in solitude, and often play better that way, it seems the fewer people around the more likely we are to play uninhibited. Who hasn't felt the nerves on the first tee at a scramble when a dozen people are watching.

Investing also is best engaged as a private matter, done in the confidence of only a few, whose judgment is trusted. There should be no competitive intentions involved. The more investing issues and decisions are made public, the more muddied the waters will become with far-flung, even contradictory input from everyone with an opinion.

Imagine Jack Nicklaus taking swing tips from people in the gallery, or Tiger Woods checking his email for fan observations on improving his tempo. Stick with your coach and your caddy. Let the scorecard do the talking. Of all the possible cast of characters you may entertain in putting together a financial team, attorney, accountant, or financial advisor, keep the following in mind:

Advice is goal oriented.

Information is market oriented.

The interpretation of information is what you are paying for. It should be based on a sound familiarity with your circumstances. Judgment and wisdom make a person successful in the long run and those qualities can be found in good advisors, coaches and caddies.

"Where no counsel is the people fall."- **Book of Proverbs.**

COURSE
MANAGEMENT

"Boy, all these people with their crackpot systems.
You listen to all of them, you'll go nuts."
- *John Updike, Playing the Game*

Before you play a round, have you ever taken the time to look over the yardage book, or if it's a familiar course, review the holes in your mind to organize some type of plan of attack? Knowing what it is you want to do and where you want the ball to go opens up a great deal of opportunities to you. It allows you to swing more freely and with some trust because you are not locked into analysis every time you step up to the ball. You're not constantly asking yourself 'What should I do now?' If you've done this kind of preparation you know what I'm talking about. It will save you from trying too hard, trying to impress your playing partners or being fixated on shooting a low number. Undoubtedly, there won't be perfection, but the results will come and will more likely be an improvement over a 'no clue' approach.

My son is going to be trying out for the high school golf team as a freshman in the fall. He has been out a number of times with me trying to hone his game, but he has actually spent most of his time at the range. This may make him a better ball striker but when it comes to a tournament or a match play event, his lack of course management experience could leave him frozen by indecision.

The best of the professional golfers transform the exercise of course management into an art form. They pick the holes where they have the best chance of making birdie and then pick clubs and distances for the sequence of shots they are going to hit. They know where a par is a good score because of the degree of difficulty and that helps to keep them from getting greedy on those holes and courting disaster. Does it work out exactly as planned? Hardly. But they know what they 'want' to do. When they get in to trouble they've got to think at least one shot ahead for the best possible results.

I remember watching Tom Lehman come down the last few holes at Torrey Pines at the 2005 Buick Invitational tied with Tiger Woods at 15 under. Lehman hit a good shot off the tee but was 30 yards behind Tiger in the fairway. He had over 260 yards from the fairway to reach the green over water, which would have been quite a stretch. So he laid up. His shot landed at exactly 88 yards from the hole which the announcer said was the perfect distance for his wedge shot. Nothing like giving yourself a great shot at birdie. It was skill and management that he put to work there. He knew the distance that would give him the best chance to score and realized his inability to hit a very long second with reliable accuracy, especially over water.

Unfortunately, PGA Tour pro's don't practice the enviable and artful use of the mulligan, which is what Tom ended up needing at that moment. He came up short on his wedge shot and proceeded to three putt, handing the victory to Tiger. That being said, it was still a fine display of course management with the minor detail of flawed execution. I suppose it could have been worse... it could have been a Tin Cup moment, or a Jean Van de Velde barefoot disaster.

It is your plan that steadies and centers your efforts. It is your plan that eases anxieties that can erupt when the unexpected happens. The same can be said for the plan in your financial life. If it is well designed and thought out it will be a guide that will calm you in turbulence and keep you from the temptation of greed. A plan will lay out what you expect so you can measure your progress against something reasonable. If you fail to have your own benchmark against which to compare you will be subject to conventional wisdom. Conventional wisdom lends itself to a herd mentality. Isn't it odd that when mutual funds or stocks experience net outflows, (people cashing out) that is almost always the best time to be putting money in?

"I remember saying to my mentor, 'If I had more

money, I would have a better plan.' He quickly responded, 'I would suggest that if you had a better plan, you would have more money.' You see, it's not the amount that counts; it's the plan that counts." - Jim Rohn

14 LIES

"All my clubs go 135 yards."
- Eugene of Norwell MA

Hey, Eugene! Something's wrong.

Imagine if everything averaged just 3%. Your bonds, your stocks, your certificates of deposit. You would eventually have to ask 'what's the deal here?'

Of course, Eugene should have been able to figure that out. I was golfing with him on the south shore of Massachusetts last winter in unseasonably mild 50 degree weather. He actually believed that all of his clubs gave him about 135 yards. A club designer would have pulled his hair out hearing that. Of the fourteen lofts, lies and lengths in his bag, he really never managed more than 135 yards each. Not all were down the middle as I came to realize. I hope you are asking yourself the same question I did. Why does Eugene carry a bag full of clubs? Maybe he should just stick with a pitching wedge, maybe a putter. Take a load off. Aren't certain instruments supposed to deliver more than others? Isn't that what we've come to expect? Isn't that what the whole risk/reward equation is about?

As golfers we are always looking for something to take a few strokes off of our score. Often, we think we're willing to do whatever it takes for improvement, looking at the conventionally obvious for answers. But a lot of the time it can be the little things that require minimum effort on our part that make a measurable difference. For instance, the new hybrid clubs, iron-woods or trouble clubs, as they are sometimes called, give us an advantage over the long irons. They are more comfortable to swing for most golfers and far more forgiving, especially out of the rough. This translates to better shots, not because our swing has improved, but because of better design and technology. At the end of the round it may mean 3 or 4 strokes less on the scorecard. What took them so long?

In the investment world there are a few changes or tweaks that could bring us better returns if we were aware of them. The conventional approach for change gets bogged down in the retail answers. The investments that are listed in the newspaper as the biggest or cheapest get the attention of the masses. However, if you were to look outside of the retail marketplace you would find the options that could add real performance to your finances.

Take for instance, the institutional fund. These often have lower operating costs than most retail funds. Their fund managers are often unavailable and unaffordable directly to the average investor. According to the USA TODAY, between 1995 and 2004 the average large company institutional fund beat the average retail fund 9.6% to 8.55% annually. Small amounts like that compounded over years can result in tens and hundreds of thousands of extra dollars in your account. (See www.NACUBO.org)

Occasionally, you can get access to these managers through pooled investments or wrap accounts where the minimum investment is not millions of dollars.

I have a friend who, until he gave up golf altogether, was a poster child for one of the worst types of golf handicaps. He had lost confidence in almost every club in his bag except his 3 iron. He would tee off with it, hit approach shots with it, chip with it, and sadly (almost desperately) hit long putts with it. He had systematically divested himself of all the other tools in his bag one by one as he lost confidence in each. He dutifully carried them around the course as though he was a real golfer. I suppose it would have looked awkward to walk the course with one club in your hand. He did not have the skill to make golf a one-club game. Of course his approach was the golf equivalent to many people's approach to their financial investments. They have a bad experience with their stock funds and they pull out. They get burned in a limited partnership and they sell off. They try a bond fund just before interest rates spike, they sell and never return. They go from 14 clubs to eight, then to five and eventually to two or three. They curl up in the fetal position clutching their certificates of deposit, savings bonds and make whimpering noises. All the while, carrying the emotional baggage of clubs that have disappointed them.

Another strange approach to the loss of confidence in your clubs is the acquisition of too many. I've watched people add all variations of investment vehicles to their 'portfolio' in an attempt to heal its wounds. They are the type who will walk into my office with 67 different mutual funds and stocks with no reasoned answer to the question 'why do you own these?' If their portfolio were a golf bag they would have to pull it with a trailer hitch. They've been swayed by every slick promotion and promise.

Tiger Woods had this to say about amateurs and their equipment selection: "They go into the golf shop, pick a club because they like the way it looks, then go to the range and hit a few shots and buy it…They may never know that the club doesn't fit them…Have your clubs fit for you."

There are sufficient considerations when getting fit for clubs: grip size, lie angle, loft, graphite or steel, shaft length and cost, among others. Your investment portfolio has its considerations as well. Even with the seemingly straight forward world of mutual funds you need to know:

Security type held – basically the stocks, bonds, cash categories or a combination thereof.

Taxability – does it kick out a lot of capital gains or dividend income or does it try to limit the tax liability (could be a function of turnover – the manager selling and buying large portions of the holdings)

Volatility – is the performance likely to be all over the map? The historical returns may not tell you what kind of a ride it took to get there. Volatility is measured by what is called standard deviation. It is the *stimpmeter* of your investments. If it rolls too fast and too far, you may never get it to the hole.

Costs – not just the asset manager's costs for running the fund, but the sales costs associated with share class (i.e. A, B, C, R – upfront, deferred, or ongoing sales charges and 12b1 fees) the internal trading costs for portfolio turnover, etc.

Overlap – it may be a good way to grip your club but it could mean you own more of the same types of securities than you think. Very often two dissimilar sounding funds can own a lot of the same stocks. That causes them to act too similar in market conditions giving you less balance and ability to weather significant downturns.

According to a recent study (by Pacific Life, 2004) jumping from one fund or index to another based on past performance can cost you a lot of money. *In fact, a diversified portfolio of indices could have made you between 18 and 32% more money over a 20 year period than trying to move from fund to fund chasing performance.*

Hole in One:

- The average player has 12,000 to 1 odds of making a hole in one.
- A PGA Tour player has 2,375 to 1 odds of making a hole in one.
- There is a five fold improvement when a pro swings the club.

150 YARDS AND IN

"Why am I using a new putter? Because the last one
didn't float too well."
-Craig Stadler

The majority of your clubs are used from 150 yards and in. The majority of your strokes come from that distance. It makes sense to get better at that part of your game.

What is the financial '150 & in'? Two things. The first is asset allocation. According to the Brinson Beebower study it accounts for about 92% of your overall performance. So picking the right asset categories to own is the key. The ancillary things like market timing and individual stock selection only contribute 7% of your total return. Asset allocation is the equivalent of getting your distances right. If you are 150 yards to the center of the green and you get it 92% right your probably *somewhere* on the green. Now let's say you've got a lag putt of twenty-five feet. Get it 92% right and you're left with a two foot tap in. Don't major in the minor issues. Spend time in the areas that deliver the biggest impact. Asset allocation is one of them.

The second thing to be concerned with is taxes. Taxes are an unrelenting pull on your assets. They should be minimized at every opportunity, however, be aware of the handcuffs that tax-deferred vehicles put on you.

Tax deferred is usually a way of saying 'no access until you are 59 ½.' They usually carry the same penalty for early withdrawal that IRA's have without the deduction going in. Tax-managed accounts on the other hand attempt to minimize taxable gains by offsetting them with available losses. They will produce taxable gains, (assuming growth) however, the taxes will be considerably less than a regular account. Tax-free accounts are obviously the most tax sensitive, yet you will give up some measure of performance to get these accounts. They are the municipal bonds whose gains are free from taxes. Their yield is inevitably less than taxable bonds. The question is, how big is the difference? If you can get a 3% yield from a tax-free municipal bond, it is roughly equivalent to getting 4% in a taxable bond and paying 25% taxes on that yield. The higher your tax bracket the more it makes sense to consider tax free municipals for your bond portion of a portfolio.

It's a little like getting strokes in match play. The more strokes you get and the better you play, the greater your chances of victory.

ARCHITECTS AND TAXES

"The income tax has made more liars out of the
American people than golf has. "
- Will Rogers, Illiterate Digest (1924)

Some of the great architects of the last century or so have left a mark on the game of golf that endures and even grows. Names like Seth Raynor, William Bell, C.B. Macdonald, Alister MacKenzie, Don Ross and A.W. Tillinghast evoke images of pipe smoking, nattily attired gentlemen from the first half of the twentieth century. Most of their designs still remain and many have become the bastion of wealth and privilege. Some thankfully are still very much in the public access domain. The 'Golden Age' of course design spanned roughly the time from the turn of the century to the beginning of World War II. As is the case with any earthly creation some have passed away, and some never came to fruition.

Have you ever grumbled or heard, "How did I get in a bunker? Nobody told me this was here! Who the heck put a *%!@^&# bunker where you can't see it from the fairway?" Could it be possible that they actually pay some sinister mind to create circumstances and conditions that cause you stress and anxiety? Could it be that you would actually pay real money to torment yourself like that? Yes and yes.

A mastermind with a team of well equipped laborers moved mountains of earth into mounds and slopes of troublesome terrain with you in mind. He is your course architect. The architect's mission is to challenge, lure, and even deceive players into taking too much club or too little club. When you've landed just off the green, but short-sided yourself, he's made sure your gentle chip will trickle 25 feet past the hole. He often gives you a sense of claustrophobia with narrow shoots off of the tee box and tight fairways. To what end? Why would he want to have such an influence on you, a perfect stranger, often many years after he's departed? The answer is clever engineering. With careful design he can cause you to aim to one side on particular shots. He can make you wish you had laid up on others. He can see to it that enough balls are available for resale in the clubhouse after you've washed yours in a pond which seemed closer than it actually was. In essence, he can exercise some control of your behavior. Or, at the very least, make you wish you had done something different.

The tax landscape is a lot like the course architect. The tax code is a study on social engineering. It rewards certain behaviors, punishes others and often causes some to wish they weren't in the game at all.

Consider deductible debt. If you buy a house you can deduct the interest on the money borrowed to purchase it. If you borrow money to buy undeveloped land, your debt is not deductible. That is a clear example of encouraging a particular behavior – owning a home. It is designed to stimulate certain sectors of the economy and certain demographics in society.

If you own certain assets long enough (usually one year or more) and then sell them at an appreciated price, the growth is taxed at a more favorable rate than ordinary earned income. It is taxed at the capital gains rates of five or fifteen percent. That is a clear incentive to buy certain types of assets with the commitment of owning them for at least a year. Stocks fall into that category, which promotes an incentive to invest for long-term purposes. Even dividends from certain domestic (U.S.) stocks receive lower tax rate treatment than dividends from foreign stocks. That invites us to invest here in America.

Payroll taxes are more easily controlled than any other tax because they can be monitored as they are earned. The burden is put on the employer to report income and do the withholding for the government. Although taxes are not due until the following year, 80% of America dutifully gives Uncle Sam the use of their money in advance. With the graduated tax rate system there is an attempt to shift some of the wealth in this country to those who do not earn enough to support themselves. There have been numerous mentions of the flat tax which would make a percentage consistent across the board for everyone. No matter how much or how little you made you would pay a predictable percentage. The more you made the more you would pay. As it stands today, however, there is more of a tax incentive to attempt to make money in an asset ownership environment than in higher wages.

The deductibility of your retirement account is also a product of some social engineering. Allow me to be a bit cynical for a moment. Why would a group of politicians, generally well-educated politicians, continue to increase the allowable deductible limits to our retirement accounts? Don't they like taxes, especially taxes due now? After all that is a large part of how they derive their power, the spending of our tax rolls on their pet projects. I'm not going to go 'conspiracy theory' on you, but could it be that there is something larger at stake here? We have all heard the issues surrounding Social Security and its eventual bankrupt status down the road. We entrust those solutions to elected officials who generally cannot agree on anything but replacing the marble tile in the congressional lavatories.

Here are the concerning numbers. Baby boomers number 77 million. There are about 38 million people behind them of sufficient age to be gainfully employed while boomers enter and linger through the typical retirement years. The math does not hold up for half as many workers to be supporting Social Security and Medicare benefits as those who are eligible to receive those benefits.

We have watched as anemic bipartisan attempts have been made to stave off the inevitable. The age at which people become eligible for Social Security has been pushed back a couple of years. No great impact there. The taxable wage base for which we all contribute our 7.65% has risen each year. However, benefits are also increasing, and Medicare's effectiveness is waning as medical costs increase at a greater pace.

The cynical view, but likely answer to the problem in the future will be to increase ordinary income taxes. Those are the taxes we will pay on our earned income as well as withdrawals from our 401k accounts, Individual Retirement Accounts, Simplified Employer Pension plans, and Tax Sheltered Annuities.

Here is the generally accepted formula which compels us to defer our income in these plans:

"I'll save 25% in taxes if I defer now, and take it out at a lower rate when I'm retired."

I've got a feeling that this plan is going to be complicated by the giant juggernaut heading our way. Imagine the uproar if they tried to take away the social programs offered. The unprepared would overload the welfare rolls in no time. It is far easier in the eyes of elected officials to gradually increase taxes on withdrawals from qualified plans. The increase in taxes on a state and local level will come partly as a result of under funded pension plans. In our little state of New Hampshire we were recently notified of a $2 billion shortfall in the system that provides for teachers, police, firefighters, state and municipal employees. Multiply that on a per capita basis across the country and you can begin to see the scope of the problem.

This impending issue is also the reason the illegal alien problem is not getting the solution most would hope for. Here are grown workers ready to assimilate into our society, and eventually onto our tax rolls without the time and discomfort of the normal birth rate curve. That border wall will get built once the tax funding equation is balanced, not before.

Seems like an appropriate time for a formula...

$$V = U*(1+e)/(1+m/M)$$

V = velocity of the ball
U = club head speed
m = mass of ball
M = mass of club head
e is the coefficient of restitution

Sorry, that was the ball speed formula. Time to simplify the Newtonian formula:

$$F=MA$$

Force equals mass times acceleration. The force of something is equal to its size, multiplied by how fast it is accelerating at you. The issues of under-funded and unfunded pensions, the Medicare funding shortfall and the expectations from Social Security and other 'entitlement' programs is so large it is hard to grasp. The exponential speed at which it is developing will surprise us all. My apologies to "Sir" Isaac for this simplistic explanation, but his one is coming at us with a lot more force than a Jason Zuback long drive tee shot.

What can you do to counter the possibility of these future changes. Consider as much 'non-qualified' investing as possible. Start the process of systematic investing in a non-deductible account with the same discipline that you should in your qualified plan. It appears from most legislative activity we have witnessed in the last 25 years that those with the most influence seem to benefit from primarily from capital gains tax treatment, not earned income tax treatment and you know they will not legislate against themselves. Secondly, if you can, get going on a Roth IRA, because they are tax deferred and come out tax free after age 59 ½. Remember that the viability of qualified accounts is greater with matching contributions.

"The difference in golf and government is that in golf you can't improve your lie."
- George Deukmejian

SO, WHAT IS PAR?

"I was three over. One over a house, one over a patio,
and one over a swimming pool."
- George Brett

Things change. That is what recent developments are for. The scores we are used to seeing by the best golfers are far beyond what the creators of the game must have envisioned. Breaking 80 at The Old Course at St. Andrews first occurred in 1858. A fellow by the name of Allen Robertson shot a 79 and things probably got pretty wild in the clubhouse. Today that wouldn't make the cut, but it probably was the equivalent of posting a news-making 59 today.

Par is a standard of excellence that we golfers shoot for when we play a hole. According to the USGA "Par is the number of strokes an excellent player should need to play a hole without mistakes under ordinary weather conditions over the average type of ground, always allowing him two putts on the green." Wouldn't we all like to be considered 'excellent'?

Here's a statistic not too many people realize. The Vardon Trophy is the honor given annually to the PGA Tour player with the lowest scoring average. (It began in 1947, prior to that it was based on points.) Who do you think is missing from the list of recipients of that award. Tiger has won it many times (five in a row at one point), Watson won it three times in a row, as did

Trevino. However, the golfer many considered to be the greatest of all time, Jack Nicklaus, never won the Vardon Trophy for the lowest scoring average. Yet he has the greatest overall record of major wins and is second in total professional tournaments won.

In fact, for the first four years of the award the scoring average was under 70. Then over the next 37 years, 31 times the average was over 70. Of course, it hasn't been over 70 since 1987 (Don Pohl has the distinction of being the last winner to average over 70.)

Par comes in different sizes. By that I mean that the length of the hole determines the par. Have you ever seen a 450 yard par 3? Of course not. A standard has been set to determine what par should be.

According to the USGA:

Par	Men	Women
3	up to 250	up to 210
4	251 to 470	211 to 400
5	471+	401+
6	576 and over	

So how do we find par in our investments? What should we be shooting for? Who sets the standard? Just as the USGA uses tens of thousands of rounds and scores to come to it's conclusions we need sources of averages to find if our investments are par or better. Unfortunately, too many have used the Standard and Poor's 500 Index as the benchmark against which they measure. The trouble with that approach is that only funds that hold those very types of stocks would be comparable. What do you measure a conservative equity-income fund against? How about a real estate sector fund or a natural resources fund? For retail funds one of the better sources of comparative measurement is Lipper Analytical. It compiles statistical returns on all types of retail fund categories and takes into account their transactional costs and fund management costs. If your fund consistently underperforms its categorical averages it's time to look elsewhere.

Exactly what par is for you is not quite as clear cut as in golf, but the sooner you identify it, the easier it will be to reach. The amount of time you have to accumulate and the target number you need are the variables that drive the process. (See *Headwinds and Tailwinds)*

As we mentioned before, the retail investment world is different from the institutional world. That world is comprised of pension and endowment fund managers. They have less transactions to be concerned with (such as constant flows from redemptions, sales and purchases.) That allows them to usually be more fully invested in the market. The availability to the returns of these funds is much less accessible to the average investor. But if we were to hold Tiger up as our standard in golf to be aspired to, then perhaps the great long-term results of the managers of the National Association of College and University Business Officers (NACUBO) could be our target to shoot for.

They are, as the name suggests, the managers of enormous endowment funds. Sure, they probably don't dress as cool and wouldn't know a wasp from the 'stinger', but they're all we've got besides Warren Buffett.

DEGREE OF DIFFICULTY

"Golf is not a game of great shots. It's a game of the most misses. The people who win make the smallest mistakes."
- Gene Littler

Ever wonder why the longer the club and lower the loft, the more difficult the club is to hit? Well according to Tom Wishon, noted club designer, there is something called the '24/38 rule'. It is a well founded belief that clubs lower than a 24 degree loft (i.e. your 3 iron and below) are not hittable with any consistency by the average golfer. It also applies to clubs with shafts longer than 38 inches. Those longer shafted, lower lofted clubs are the ones we spray all over the course. They cost us strokes as we attempt to recover from their (our) errancy.

That degree of difficulty carries over into investing in various ways. Consider the US equities market as the club you hit most consistently. Only occasionally does it let you down. You feel most comfortable and familiar with it. If you've got your broad market covered in a well diversified portfolio it won't carry a degree of difficulty that is impossible to handle. On the other hand, the low lofted clubs of emerging markets, commodities or options are the parts of the investable world that most cannot manage well. Pulling a club out of the bag that has not been used in quite a while requires some reacquainting. Coaches can help you master those clubs and help you determine when they should or should not be used.

It is enough of a challenge to master the tools in the bag, but that is not where the challenge ends. The ups and downs of market conditions can be like playing a round of mountain golf. Every lie seems to be uneven giving you adjustments that you are not familiar with. Ball below the feet, side hill lies, down hill lies all make the execution of your shot more challenging than usual. The objective is finding the flattest spot on the fairway and that is accomplished with broad diversification. Some portfolios carry far too few equities, and most of them perform much too similarly. Consequently, any market movement can make your portfolio move in lock-step with some narrow index. Consider the benefits of fundamental passive index investing. The broad diversification of owning most of the market with selected weightings keeps you from the wild swings and having to make your next shot from the poorest and most difficult lies.

THE GAME OVERSEAS

I remember a very successful investor back in the mid 1980's saying this about international investing – 'Trying to have a well balanced portfolio without foreign stocks is like trying to write a letter with only half of the alphabet.'

In 1816 golfers had four choices of clubs: spoons, scrapers, light irons, and heavy irons. For about a century the choices didn't improve too much. As recently as 1977 we had only four real TV channels and one method of shipping a document across the country. Choice is now almost more of a challenge than a convenience. Globalization has magnified that challenge.

Most golfers know the TaylorMade brand. In fact, I own some of their clubs and love them. Yet because we see a company as a domestic one listed on the New York Stock Exchange or the NASDAQ we may assume that it is affected by domestic issues only. Consider that TaylorMade's drivers are only assembled in the USA. Their driver heads and shafts are made in China. Most major companies have some form of international component to them.

Owning a foreign stock or a domestic one with considerable international ties make it subject to a lot of considerations...fluctuating currency rates, shipping conditions affected by weather, terror, tariff changes, labor disputes and governmental instability. Knowing your investment's foreign profile is a bit more difficult than reading the label on your golf club, but the sources of information are available. Be sure to understand the international implications of your stock ownership.

GOLF BALLS AND MUTUAL FUNDS

How much does the average golfer know about the various types of golf balls? How would he know if it were the proper ball for him? Does his skill level even warrant the discussion?

Golf balls come in three basic constructions:

- Two piece
- Three piece
- Four piece

Not many amateurs can tell you the difference between them.

Allegedly, the two-piece gives you more distance and is more durable. The three piece presumably allows for more spin and control. The four piece must have a solid core of Viagra to increase the time it stays aloft. Of course, in the rare occurrence that it should stay aloft for more than four hours, please call The Golf Channel.

Marketing golf balls is, at times, a loss leader. It does not generate the profits for most companies that other equipment sales do. In fact, some companies won't enter the fray because of the costly process and necessary advertising expense. (Have you seen a PING ball that has made it to market?) Last season's novelty in the golf ball segment is in this season's bargain bin and not necessarily because of quality. More than likely it just couldn't keep the consumer's attention.

The mutual fund industry is guilty of some of the same practices. A company with sufficient name recognition creates a niche fund following a hot trend and collects assets. Most of the assets are coming from other funds. It's not new money. According to Mark Riepe, in the August 2006 *Journal of Financial Planning*, during the years of 1994-2001 there were 300 instances where a mutual fund company changed its name to either reflect a popular style of investing or to avoid an unpopular style. They didn't change any aspect of their actual investment activity, just the name. Investors poured an additional $18 billion into those funds compared with their peer funds. Most of it is money in transition, moving from one company to another, with the assumption that the performance will be better. The largely unanswered question for the consumer is, "What makes this fund better than the last?"

It's like the golf ball, slick white on the outside with a mystery core always promising more distance and greater control. The retail financial consumer drives this process day after day, chasing the 'hot dot' on the fund chart. Financial product providers target these people because they represent a possibility of net inflow to them. The application of the Pareto Principle is at work. All they need is 20 percent of a market to participate and they will generate 80 percent of the revenues.

The golf industry also recognizes its best clientele.

You are probably among them. They are what the National Golf Foundation calls the 'core golfers'. They achieve that designation by crossing the threshold of playing at least eight full rounds per year. The average rounds played is likely much higher. There are reportedly about 13 million golfers in this core group. That is less than half of the total estimated players of the game. Yet those 47 percent account for over 90 percent of the total rounds played and 87 percent of the golf related spending. You're walking around with a target on your back.

3, 6 AND 10 FOOTERS

"The only real misfortune, the only real tragedy,
comes when we suffer without learning the lesson."
- Emmet Fox

I don't know about you, but as a kid, my mother tried to tell me, as my wife does today that 'it's the little things that count.'

Does it not seem completely incongruous that a drive of 310 yards (930 monstrous manly feet) counts as much as a three foot putt? All the excitement seems to be on the tee box while all the stress is on the putting green. Why is that?

It's the finish work. It's the margin for error. I do not mind participating in a small construction project as long as the only skill required is banging nails and cutting things 'roughly this long.' As I think about it, destruction is more in line with my skill set. Try to get me to do the finish work and it'll look like high school woodshop gone horribly wrong. I can miss the center of the fairway by twenty yards and not be too concerned, but be two inches off line on the putt and you start adding them up quickly.

The big hits get all the brief glory. The big moves in the portfolio get all the attention. What gets you a good score are the short shots. In the investment world, it is called rebalancing.

Rebalancing is far from glamorous. It's the consistent working of the short game. It is the systematic moving out of winners in small percentages and into laggards, bringing everything back into a proper allocation. It is so counterintuitive that it hurts. Almost no one does it consistently without some automated program in place because thinking about it invites emotion. 'Tell me why I want to do this again? I am supposed to sell the good performers and buy the poor performers? And how much do I pay you?'

Did you know that a study conducted by T. Rowe Price showed that rebalancing quarterly could end up improving your average return by almost one percent over long periods of investing?

Do you want 8 percent or 9 percent? Do you want to shoot 85 or 75? Working on you putting stroke is almost as glamorous, but it could have the same impact on your game.

THE SCORING CLUBS

'He hit more lips than a drunk dentist.'

As a golfer you most certainly read or heard of the three clubs that are considered scoring clubs. Although some would include the pencil, there appears to be a consensus that the clubs are the driver, the wedge and the putter. These clubs account for close to 75 percent of the average golfer's total strokes. The desire to master those clubs would seem to be critical. Reasonable accuracy with those clubs offers a high probability of avoiding wild swings in your hole to hole scoring. Getting to the short grass accurately, avoiding three putts, etc. are the staples of good scoring. Unfortunately, too many golfers spend time on the driver to exclusion of the others. Or similarly, they reach for a seldom used club, perhaps a two or three iron, at a critical stage of their game hoping to pull of a shot.

As in golf, investing has its three fold scoring focal points. The first is the fact that stocks outperform bonds over almost every meaningful and measurable time horizon. A portfolio that is to gain ground in real wealth terms will have to incorporate a reasonable percentage of equities.

Secondly, the long term consistent out-performance of value stocks over growth stocks is a fundamental premise to the construction of a portfolio. (The

University of Chicago, Center for Research in Security Prices bears out these facts with its academic approach to broad historical performance.)

Third, is the sometimes uncomfortable but nevertheless provable fact that small cap equities need to be a part of a stock portfolio in percentages roughly between 10 and 20 percent. Their volatility, when taken separately, keeps most investors away, but the alchemy of asset class combinations including small cap stocks is undeniable. In fact, between 1970 and 2002, adding a 30 percent international small cap exposure to an otherwise one hundred percent S&P 500 portfolio could slightly reduce overall volatility and increase it's return by eighteen percent. It seems incongruous, but it is true.

So there are your investment scoring clubs:

- incorporating a substantial percentage of stocks in a portfolio
- leaning toward value stocks
- including small cap stocks (of both value and growth styles)

POSTAGE STAMPS AND PRIZE MONEY

"Money is better than poverty, if only for the financial reasons."
- Woody Allen

The year is 1986. Corey Pavin wins in Milwaukee. His first place prize money is $72,000.

1996 - Ten years later, Corey wins again. Who would have imagined that first place prize money could have swollen to $270,000?

2006 – Corey comes out of a long winless streak to take the US Bank tournament in Milwaukee. He wins $720,000. (Had he won any of the majors in 2006 he would have earned over $1.25 million.)

Twenty years of golfing and a ten fold increase in prize money.

- Arnold Palmer in 1963 was the first to reach $100,000 in a single season.
- Curtis Strange in 1988 surpassed $1 million dollars in a season.
- Tiger Woods, 1997 first to win $2 million dollars in a season.
- Vijay Singh in 2004, the first to win $10 million dollars in a single season.

A quick look at the average wage in the US and we

can see that income has not had the same bump upwards. Sure you say, golf acquired Tiger Woods and the curve of prize money shot upwards. Well, that is true, but the economy had its share of upward pressure too. We had the internet boom, productivity improvements from technology, global economic trade, and a service economy that justified its non-manufacturing wages.

In the summer of 1975 I could send a letter for 10 cents. As of 2007 it was 42 cents. Same service, nothing greatly improved about it, just getting a one ounce letter from here to there. If a postage stamp is a good barometer of my actual cost of living, then how will I fare in retirement when my earned income ceases, and my investments are left to do all the heavy lifting?

Cost of living is your slope rating. It is your degree of difficulty. The higher the number, the greater the challenge of getting to par. If inflation is running high, it is that much more difficult to outpace with investments, especially certain types of investments.

How often have you heard reports of the inflation rate? It is reported as the Consumer Price Index and is tracked by the Federal Reserve Bank of New York. What we get as a figure revolves largely around workers. That is to say that the index is weighted according to the relative importance of different categories which are pertinent to the average working person. For example, energy costs, transportation, medical care costs among others are all given certain percentage weightings. Averaged together they comprise the CPI.

However, what most people are unaware of is the fact that the government has been tracking another CPI rate for quite some time now. It is what they refer to as the CPI-E. The E stands for elderly, which they define as 62 and over. That index has different weightings because different factors generally play different roles in the lives of those over that age. Health care costs are more heavily weighted, as are housing costs. Transportation plays a smaller role because of reduced commuting, etc. Since the early 1980's that CPI has been tracking about 12 percent higher. Thru 2001 it was 3.38 percent versus 3 percent. What does that do to your purchasing power over 25 years?

3 percent	3.38 percent
$50,000/yr today	$50,000/yr today
$104,500/yr (25 yrs)	$115,000/yr (25 yrs)

It doesn't seem like a great increase but what you need to consider is that in order to keep up with their inflation the elderly will have to get higher returns. How is that usually done? By taking on more risk. Are the elderly inclined to do that?

Here is the next issue. There is also an estimate for the boomer generation. They constitute such a large percentage of the population that they are being tracked separately. The estimate for boomers because of their lifestyle choices and reticence to give them up, is *a concerning 4.5 percent.* That is fully fifty percent higher than the reported CPI. That will push today's $50,000 need to $150,250 in 25 years. That is a tripling of necessary income during retirement.

The generation that 'wants it all' is going to have to figure out a way to keep it all. There will be fewer workers, therefore less productivity. (See Shooting Your Age.) Consumer purchases will be fewer. Taxes from workers will have to support ever enlarging programs. But I digress...quite possibly into a political tirade. So much for senior discounts.

RISK / REWARD RELATIONSHIP

There is always free cheese in a mousetrap.

HEADWINDS AND TAILWINDS

"The older you get the stronger the wind gets--and it's always in your face."
- Jack Nicklaus

If you love golf you will play it in all kinds of weather. Postal workers could learn a thing or two from the passionate golfer about braving the elements. The conditions we encounter will not only alter the way our ball travels, but it will also play with our head and cause us to do things we shouldn't do. Headwinds and tailwinds always tend to make us reckless. With a headwind you tend to over-swing so as not to be short. With a tailwind you're thinking you can make the hole so much shorter with a monster drive, so you leave your shoes and most likely the fairway. When you begin to have exaggerated expectations you lose your points of reference. What you thought was an unreachable par five can falsely appear to be an eagle opportunity. Your fear of carrying over water into a headwind can get you to completely change the tempo of your swing…and there go your results, splash!

In our recent memory we have both types of financial events to learn from. The decade of the nineties was a tailwind like we had not seen in the last 50 years. The carelessness that came with that period of time gradually built upon itself and eventually caught a lot of people blindsided. The presumption of anything short of a 20% return being unacceptable was quite widespread. I had conversations with people who actually thought that business fundamentals had changed forever. Profits weren't necessary to carry a company, just the potential for them some day was enough. Dotcoms offered a new paradigm that was getting a relatively few people rich on the speculation and misinformation of many. It was as if bogeys were a thing of the past and birdies were the new par.

The headwinds we've experienced have been fewer in number but no less damaging to our psyches. Our tailwind of the nineties was like playing a links course, getting unbelievable distance on our shots only to turn back into an unforgiving gale force wind. The expectations of your distance were gone. Your driver went as far as a normal 7 iron. The three years of 2000 through 2002 got progressively worse as far as expectations go. Returns in the overall stock market were deeply in the negative double digits, and your opportunities to bail out for something safe were unpalatable. 'Safe' money returns in savings accounts dropped to a fraction of a percent, and the historically safe money market funds actually had net losses after expenses were subtracted. The harsh whiplash effect of moving spastically from the 1990's tailwind to the headwind of the new century left many people wanting to throw out their scorecards.

Aggressiveness off the tee can lead you to be very conservative on your next shot. Imagine you decide to pull out the driver on the tee. You bend it into the woods. Now you are stuck behind some trees with a decision to make. You could make a terrible mess of things. Do you punch out conservatively to have a shot at the green? Do you take a drop? Can you? What are the penalties associated with your compromised position?

Your assumption of returns, and therefore, your selection of investment vehicle is like the tee shot. Ten percent, twelve percent, or more, as an expected long term return is tempting. Here is how the aggressive play can turn you conservative, and vise versa.

In order to accumulate half a million dollars over a 20 year period of time you must save:

If you earn:	
Monthly	**Percent**
$690	10%
$875	8%
$1,100	6%

10 percent is tempting. It's the same feeling you get when you try to reach the long par 5 in two. It probably requires two exceptional shots. In your mind it is possible. Is it probable? Be honest.

If you are conservative in your return assumptions (i.e. 6 percent) you will have to be aggressive with your savings pace ($1,100/month). If you take the more conservative monthly savings amount ($690/month) you will have to be more aggressive with your investments.

Fast forward to retirement. You decided to invest $690 per month with an assumption of 10 percent. You actually got 6 percent. Now you have to be aggressive. You will have call upon all of your job interview skills to out-position yourself against all of the sixteen year old grocery baggers. Conversely, you decided to invest $1,100 per month with an assumption of only 6 percent. You actually got 8 percent return. Now you've got a couple of extra years of freedom, a couple of extra weeks a year in Aruba. Nicely done.

Better to be aggressive with what you can control and be a realist with what you cannot.

INFOMERCIALS & DISCLOSURES:

"Golf isn't like a sitcom, where problems are presented in the first five minutes, then solved in the last five minutes."
- Olin Browne

The financial industry is full of disclosures. There is a constant heaping on of mounds of prospectuses, volumes of fine print, and suitability information to assure the 'proper fit' for an investment and the consuming investor. Unfortunately in the end, most of the effort expended to give full disclosure is nothing more than a documented effort to CYA (cover your ass, for those who just came ashore.) There are good reasons to ask all those questions and compile all that information. Should an investor with only ten thousand dollars to invest begin with an aggressive hedge fund? Of course not. It all boils down to suitability. What fits well versus what constricts your breathing? With every broker, brokerage house and mutual fund institution under growing scrutiny we would hope that some of the glitzy promotion and promissory language that have tempted so many should be replaced with the truth. Wouldn't it be nice to boil it down to the common sense maxim, "if it seems to good to be true, it probably is." It just sounds so darn good. Consider it the equivalent of financial Viagra – if the reports of its performance seems too inflated for more than four hours (or four months, or four years) consult a professional.

No matter how late at night it is, no matter how long it takes to fumble for your credit card to call that number on the screen, or how many cocktails you've had, no club is going to transform you into a golf genius. No club will be used for 'virtually' every shot. Neither will any investment be the balm that heals your previous neglect or puts you on easy street overnight. Have you ever stopped to think of all the investment gurus that have passed through your television channels or radio stations and are now gone. Do you think it was their investment strategy which they so altruistically shared which made them rich? Or was it the fact that they sold enough tapes and CDs and held enough seminars to fund their own early (or desperately late) retirement? There are a lot of garage sales with deeply discounted, late night program golf equipment on the cheap. Let them make the mistakes, then give them five bucks for it. Which brings me to another topic – *financial pornography.*

FINANCIAL PORN

"A magazine is simply a device to induce people to
read advertising."
-James Collins (Harper Collins)

Like it's not too distant cousin, financial porn is tempting, often twisted information packaged in a way to appeal to one of the basest of human qualities – greed. Probably one of the most shocking and disappointing sights is a bare mutual fund without the benefit of it's advertising makeup and a little digital airbrushing. Digging below the surface can uncover the real fund and it's expenses. Hyperbole will sell, but it won't get you to your destination. Try personalfund.com to find out what your real costs are.

What is the primary job of a financial magazine? Is it to counsel you personally with an intimate knowledge of your distinct circumstances or to sell as many issues as possible, while stuffing its pages with advertising like a pork sausage? You may occasionally and quite accidentally find a worthwhile tidbit of information or a helpful website somewhere wedged between their pages. But how do they get your attention? How about those cover pages?

'10 Stocks You <u>MUST</u> Own Right Now'   OR

'Best Funds to Own in the Next 12 Months'

Actually, the track records of some of the more popular financial magazines are absolutely abysmal. I refer to their investment record, because their subscription track records can be quite healthy. In fact, the vast majority of the 'best' funds listed in their pages averaged in the bottom 30% the following year. That is an approach called 'chasing the hot dot.' If you were to monitor these magazines for the exact opposite reasons you would probably make out pretty well. If you happened to own any of the funds they tell you to 'buy now' that is probably a pretty good time to sell them.

The rules governing what a magazine or newspaper can tell consumers are almost non-existent. An individual broker, planner or advisor saying the same thing is held to a much higher standard.

According to DALBAR's "Quantitative Investor Behavior" study (reported in 2004), the S&P 500 Index returned 13% from 1984 to 2003, yet the average equity investor's return was a mere 3.5% over the same period. That is due in large part to the fact that the average equity investor holds his investment for only 3.3 years. That is hardly a long term mindset. It is the product of a distracted marketplace full of major efforts to get your attention and money.

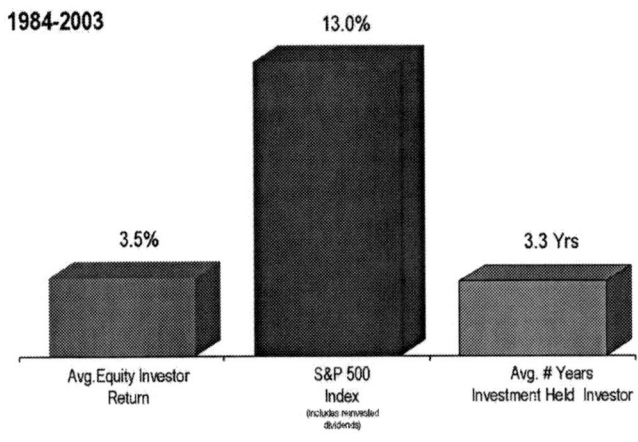

1984-2003

Avg.Equity Investor Return: 3.5%

S&P 500 Index (includes reinvested dividends): 13.0%

Avg. # Years Investment Held Investor: 3.3 Yrs

Source. DALBAR, 2004

Take a look at Morningstar for example. It's very popular rating system of stars (one star being poor and five stars being the best) came under scrutiny some years ago. Morningstar weathered those challenges well, but consider the implications of acquiring just one or two additional stars. How much do you think it is worth to a fund company to have that fifth star? Possibly hundreds of millions of new investment dollars. Those five stars in an advertising campaign are absolutely huge. They won't tell you anything about a funds performance next year. Of course, the reason the star system is so popular is its simplicity. It cuts to the heart of what people want – simplification. There is far too much noise and distraction in the investment marketplace. Staying focused is a great asset.

ME & MRS. JONES

"Golf is a game in which the slowest people in the world are those in front of you, and the fastest are those behind."
- Anonymous

I love the TV commercial where the guy is riding his lawn mower, explaining how he has a big new house with a swimming pool in a great neighborhood, and membership to the country club, etc, and then he asks rhetorically, 'how do I do it?...

I'm in debt up to my eyeballs…somebody help me.'

He is far from being alone. The national savings rate spent a brief time in the negative recently, a trend we can all hope doesn't continue. I am certain we did not all take our training from the golf course marshal who admonishes us to 'keep up with the group in front of you.' But in the interest of keeping up the pace of play we all look to the group ahead to see if we are on pace and we get a little clenched up when the group behind us seems to be pushing us.

So it is with the psychology of acquisition. How many people buy a bigger flat panel TV because their friend or neighbor did? Too many. How many buy, or more likely lease the next biggest model vehicle because someone in their social circle did? Too many.

Hummers seem to be the quintessential expression of 'look at me' cars. It must be some measure of manhood inferiority. Bigger houses, bigger cars, bigger drivers, putters, pimped out golf carts, you name it. As long as the Jones' are out there leveraging themselves there will be people following on their heels, saving nothing, sending that long-range message to the public, 'when all this rusts away, you will have to feed and clothe me because I couldn't control myself.'

SHOOTING YOUR AGE

"Age is not a particularly interesting subject. Anyone can get old. All you have to do is live long enough."
- Groucho Marx (1890 - 1977)

More than any other in history, those living in this generation have the best chance of shooting their age. Sound good? Sure it does. But it won't be because you'll bring your score down. No, you'll probably catch up to your score sooner than you'll break par.

The average male at age 65 has a fifty percent chance of living past age 85. Can you picture that? Half of the retired guys in the Tuesday afternoon league will still be around past eighty-five. And you thought they played slow now. That same average 65 year old male has a twenty five percent chance of living past 92! Now we're talking my scoring range.

Here's another way of thinking about it. You have planned and budgeted for a two week vacation then suddenly and without notice you are told you'll be given a total of five weeks of vacation. At first it sounds like great news. Then you realize you've got to get the two weeks of money to last five weeks.

According to GOLFWORLD Magazine Sept 23, 2005: a study conducted by Nationwide Financial and Golf Digest Companies found:

- 85% of golfers can tell you the score they shot for their last round, however only 52% can tell you the current value of their investments.
- 74% have increased their investment into golf related activities compared with 54% who increased the amount they regularly save for retirement.
- 94% know what areas of their game need improvement, only 45% can tell you which areas of their investment strategy require improvement.

If the financial awareness level would approach the game awareness level, golfers would be the most successful and best prepared retirees on the planet.

Longevity did not just arrive on the scene. It's been around for a long time. Thomas Jefferson and John Adams lived well into their early eighties. They were on the far end of the age curve as were many of the wealthy of their day. What has helped the average life expectancy to shoot so high so fast is the accessibility of better food, better working conditions and better medical care. Infant mortality, which has the highest impact on the averages, has greatly improved over the last fifty years.

The average have been the beneficiaries of what was the privilege of the wealthy.

When President Ronald Reagan was born the average life expectancy for an adult male was in the early fifties. Reagan made it to his mid-nineties, although the quality of his last 10 years was questionable.

In 1950 there were 2,300 people age 100 or older. There are 85,000 today. No wonder Willard Scott had to stop saying 'Happy Birthday', he was running out of time. It is estimated that by the year 2050 there will be almost 1.3 million centenarians. Worldwide, over the last 200 years, the average life expectancy has increased from 38 to 65. Consider this statistic: According to the United Nations, in 2005 16.7 percent of the U.S. population was over 60 years old. By the year 2050 an estimated 26.4 percent will be over age 60. Why? Because the boomer generation is passing through the pipeline. There are fewer people behind them.

It is not that a 'long life' has gotten much longer, it is that the average is moving up and the disparity is narrowing.

Look at the affect Tiger had on the PGA Tour. He dominated for a stretch of years. His fitness regimen made every other golfer look like the Pillsbury Doughboy. Eventually, the idea of being a fit athlete in order to compete became a necessity and expectations have risen for the so-called 'middle-aged' golfer. The growing number of over 40 golfers who can still compete on the tour now increases every year. Careers have been extended making the transition to the Champions (over 50) Tour more of an option than a necessity.

What does this mean for golfers and non-golfers alike?

It means in all likelihood, the length of time you will spend in 'retirement' will be considerably longer than the beliefs we have held.

Your savings rate and investment approach is going to be what fuels that entire time span. The average American's savings rate has dipped from 10.4% in 1980 to an all-time low today of below 1% and the pressure that will put on individuals to catch up will be enormous. I'd like to blame the banks and credit card companies for issuing access to credit so easily, but it is the consumer's choice ultimately.

Very often people confuse access to money with actually having money.

As they say, payback is a ...well, tough. It won't be long before the difference between having and having access will be made clear.

Another consideration for living as long as the Tuesday afternoon league is the eventuality of long-term care needs. Nursing home costs have risen at more than twice the cost of living rate and the national average for a year in a nursing home has pushed over $50,000. Your alternatives for paying are fairly clear cut: pay with your own cash, pay an insurance company to take the risk, or have so little money that Uncle Sam will pick up the tab with Medicaid. All of those alternatives leave a bad taste in your mouth, so don't hold out hope that there will be a tastier choice. Of course you could just drive your golf cart into the water hazard and skip the nursing home altogether.

A golfer visiting a course was assigned an 80 year old caddie, but the pro assured him that the old man's vision was perfect.

The golfer's first tee shot fades deep into the rough.

"Did you see it?" the golfer asked the caddie as they walk off the tee.
"Yup," says the old caddie with some confidence.

"Well, where is it?" he asked.

"I can't remember."

KNOWING YOUR CARRY

"You are meant to play the ball as it lies, a fact that may help to touch on your own objective approach to life."
- Grantland Rice

When you put yourself in the wrong spots on the golf course the trouble just compounds itself. Knowing the yardage of your clubs and your yardage to the hole is a key to staying out of trouble.

Surveying the hole, tee to green will help you figure out where the best landing area is, preferably where it's wide and not narrow. Some of the worst mental errors take place with unrealistic good intentions. An example of that would be an attempt to steer away from something you probably couldn't reach anyway…water at 280 yards or traps at 285 when your drive, under the best conditions would go 260. Most golfers, according to a study done by Frankly Golf, overestimate their driving distance by 30 yards. The trouble and the perception of its proximity, causes you to change your swing.

The objective is to give yourself the best conditions for a shot to the green. That involves short grass, not rough. The order of preference would be – short grass, rough, sand, water.

Knowing what you need to have at retirement is the

key to preparation. Having a realistic understanding of what inflation will do to your needs is a fundamental. Here is a formula to use. In today's dollars figure out how much you would need annually to be comfortable. Be sure to determine whether you are intending on getting Social Security. If you factor it in, subtract it from this formula. For easy math, let's pick $50,000 not including Social Security. Inflation could average anything, but let's work with 3% and 4%. Choose how many years until you retire and then find the amount you will need then <u>for every $10,000</u> you would need <u>in today's dollars.</u>

	@3%	@4%
10 yrs	**$13,440**	14,802
15 yrs	**15,580**	18,009
20 yrs	**18,061**	21,911
25 yrs	**20,938**	26,658
30 yrs	24,273	32,434

So with our $50,000 example, figuring a 4% inflation rate, retiring in 20 years we would require $21,911(per $10k) x 5 = $109,555. So, that is your need annually.

Now, how much do you need to have as a critical mass to generate that amount? All studies indicate that in order to have the best chance of sustaining your retirement income for at least 25 years, you should not withdraw at more than a 5% pace. Here's the calculation:

$109,555 divided by .05 (5% pace) = $2,191,100.

That's the nest egg requirement in 20 years. Time to pull out the scoring clubs and get to work?

HANDICAPS: TO HAVE OR HAVE NOT

A twosome leaves the 1ˢᵗ tee at 1:00 traveling at the speed of a 25 handicap. A foursome leaves the 1ˢᵗ tee at 1:10 traveling at the speed of a 12 handicap. At what hole should the twosome let the foursome play through?

Have you ever played a game called 'Chicago'? Here is how it works: each player is given a negative quota of points called a 'hurdle'. Scratch golfers get -39, a one handicap gets -38, a two handicap get -37, and so on, all the way to the 36 handicap who get -3. Then, based on their performance, players receive positive points for scoring bogeys (1 point), pars (2 points), birdies (4 points), eagles (8 points). The player who is closest to erasing or surpassing their handicap hurdle rate by the most points wins.

Hurdle rates in investing begin with your tax bracket and also factor in inflation. So if inflation is at 3% and your tax bracket is 25%, you need to make more than 4% to have any actual growth of purchasing power in your portfolio. Example: a 4% return minus 25% to taxes = 3%. If inflation is at three percent, your net 'real growth' is zero.

As we mentioned before, the projected CPI-B (for Boomers) is estimated at 4.5%. These numbers have to be factored into your retirement projections or your solutions will become problems. It has been my experience that those who keep track of what they do seem to be the ones who make measurable improvements. Those golfers who track an official handicap tend to be better golfers than those who do not. The investors who track their real progress consistently, seem to do better than those who ignore it.

You are going to need better returns and lower costs.

10, 20, 30 BEST DAYS

'Nutted it!'
– Roy McAvoy, in the movie Tin Cup

We have all hit the sweet spot and striped one down the fairway. It jazzes us up and causes us to walk taller. We just don't know when it is going to happen. Play long enough and you will experience your own 'great shot hall of fame.' As time goes by, the best ones continue to stand out in our mind. The numbers may get smaller but the quality increases. We may even save the score card because some days are better than others.

In investing the old saw goes something like this: 'It's time *in* the market, not *timing* the market,' that counts. As in golf, some days in the market stand out from others. They can have such an impact that their absence causes a significant change in your performance.

Here is an idea of what the results would have been for a lengthy period invested in the Dow Jones Industrials:

- All trading days   = 9.7%
- Minus 10 best days = 7.2%
- Minus 20 best days = 5.4%
- Minus 30 best days = 3.9%
- Minus 40 best days = 2.4%
- Minus 50 best days = 1.2%

From 9/30/1981 through 12/31/2004. [2,628 trading days] (Source: Zweig Consulting, LLC)

So what is the point? You have got to stay invested because you don't know when the next best day is coming. You have got to grind it out, because you never know when you are going to hit it on the screws and stick it a few inches from the pin.

A HUMMER IN THE TRAILER PARK

'The world is full of winners and losers. Here's hoping you're one of 'em.' - Norm Petersen (Cheers)

Jim Rohn once said that being poor is a terrible thing. It is one of the worst conditions to be in, unless you're sick. Now being poor and sick is a horrible place to be in life, unless of course you are stupid. Poor, sick and stupid - that has got to be about as far as you can fall in life…unless you're ugly.

Is there anything sadder on the golf course than the guy who couldn't find a fairway with a compass, toting in his new bag filled with a $1500 set of new golf clubs. You are so tempted to ask him 'was that a swing or a stroke?' We've all seen someone like this. It is a convoluted way of improving one's game. It's not unlike the guy who knows he's got to get going with his retirement plan, so he takes the plunge and buys 100 shares of WorldCom at its peak. Two weeks ago he was nowhere on his trip to retirement and in two weeks he will be nowhere still. What should he have done? Take lessons! Seek out professional help, even if he is paying just to ask questions.

Our friend with the bag of new clubs could have spent his money more wisely on lessons. He won't break 100 with those clubs, and he won't break 100 without some good solid advice. I have an acquaintance just like that. I'd give you his name, but he knows where I live. Besides he once shot his neighbor's dog just because it relieved itself on his lawn, so he's not too well adjusted. We'll call him Gary.

Gary, last season, went all out. He had grown tired of the yard sale menagerie of clubs he carried around in his tattered old bag. He joined a beautiful club nearby, bought the top of the line set of clubs and golfed, and golfed, and golfed some more. In fact, he had 43 full rounds logged in by the end of July (no small feat in northern New England.)

I had a chance to golf with him in mid-summer and watched as Mr. Premium Brand struggled to a 110. He hadn't dropped below his 23 handicap. All that golf, all that money, all that time, and his greatest achievement was that he hadn't lost his job. (Which remains a mystery to this day.)

It is far better to be informed and not operating under misconceptions or false assumptions. Gary thought new clubs would fix his game. He sought pleasant methods over pleasant results. He wanted an easy solution to a problem which was going to take some effort to change. He had no plan, just a credit card. New clubs may have been part of 'a' plan, probably the last part, once all the flaws and habits were uncovered. Without an understanding of the problems, new clubs will do just as poorly as old clubs.

Changing brokerage houses, stocks, going to cheaper trades, buying and selling based more on emotion than reason, etc. are all the same as buying new clubs without the diagnosis and remedy of coaching.

'HEY, ROCKY, WATCH ME PULL A RABBIT OUT OF MY HAT.'
- Bullwinkle J. Moose

The moose never got it quite right. He had the magician's hat, the magic words, the rolled up sleeve, and presto! Still no rabbit. Sometimes out on the course you feel like the moose. The club feels awkward in your hands, the swing seems uncomfortable, and if you let it bother you enough it could become a horror show. But going through the motions, doing the routine, and just paying attention to the fundamentals every time, you'll find that eventually you pull out some good shots. Do you know what I mean? Nothing feels like it should but the results just happen. You get on the green in two, but if you went by how it felt, you should have been in the woods. Trusting your swing and your routine eventually brings you out of it.

There are times when your investment results just surprise you. You feel by all accounts that nothing should be happening. Given the circumstances you think results are going to be tough, you're going to have to grind it out for a while. But, strangely, what you get sometimes is good stuff. How does it happen? By sticking to the fundamentals, staying invested instead of letting your feelings or guesses get in your way. Keep your allocation, keep rebalancing, and keep swinging.

RETIRING TO THE WRONG COURSE

"In thirty years I don't know where I'll be, but I hope
I'm happy and I hope I don't have gas."
- Billy Crystal

Pines, Creeks, Palms and Peaks…Ever notice how the names of so many golf courses all sound so similar?

Suppose you are short hitter with a fear of water hazards (see Glossary of Fear.) Now imagine that you just plunked down a nice chunk of cash for a lovely home along the fairway of a popular upscale golf course. Once your furniture has been unpacked you dig out the clubs, head to the first tee only to find that almost every hole on this course requires a carry over water or has water running the length of the fairway. What's your reaction?

Your right, you wouldn't move in without knowing a little more about the course. If golf was such a compelling reason for you to be there you would have done your homework. Do you know how many people every year head to some retirement location in another state to make it their home? They have spent the last 35 years familiarizing themselves with the tax landscape of their home location, only to trade it for a relative unknown with a very different tax structure.

For instance, Oregon's tax structure is friendly toward retirement income, but unfriendly with it's taxation of real property. Illinois gets poor marks for it's taxation of retirement income, but good marks for it's taxation of earned income. My home state of New Hampshire gets great marks for its treatment of earned income (no income tax) but only average marks on its real property taxes (public school funding presently comes exclusively from property taxes.) According to the National Association of Realtors Baby Boomers (those born between 1946 and 1964) own 57% of all the seasonal and vacation homes, and in 2005 39.9% of all residential real estate transactions were second home purchases.

Here is another issue to consider. Most of the states are governed by common law; however, some states are referred to as community property states. The rules in those states may divide or distribute your property differently at your death so, before you head out to some other state and make it your permanent residence, know how it is going to treat the assets you bring. Otherwise, bring your ball retriever.

5 BASIC SWING
FLAWS
TO RETIREMENT

"I have never thought simple enjoyment was one of the underlying virtues of the game. Golf is a damned struggle, and sometimes the struggle is defeating and sometimes it's depressing and sometimes it's encouraging and occasionally it's exhilarating."
- Michael Bamberger, "To the Linksland"

Every magazine you pick up regarding golf inevitably has an article that speaks accusingly to most of us. Usually, those of us inclined toward denial flip feverishly past those pages and on to the less critical, more palatable information. I refer, of course, to the ever disparaging, unrelenting, fault-finding article addressing swing flaws. Always full of pictures showing posed perfection opposite the contorted, clearly uncoordinated exaggerations that we fear may look like us in mid-swing.

These are the common swing flaws and the difficulty most of us have is that the pictures rarely translate well to our sense of 'feel' and 'touch'. Who can objectively tell us where we are a mess? A snapshot just won't do it justice. A good deal of it must come from our own time spent with club in hand.

So it is with some of the more abstract elements of our hopes and desires for retirement. Seeing the bigger picture and visualizing the end product is a difficult exercise for most.

NUMBER ONE: EMOTIONAL PAYOFF

"If you watch a game, it's fun. If you play it, it's recreation. If you work at it, it's golf."
- Bob Hope

Most people have spent their time in a career enjoying much more than the money they received. The feeding of our ego by way of recognition is one of the primary reasons we engage in some occupation. It is a nurturing through attention that strangely builds, even more so, as retirement approaches. The discussion of retirement's approach brings with it a built in sense of recognition, acknowledgement, and even entitlement in some cases. We have put in our time, achieved a level of competence, and served the economic machine.

As in golf, we want to do more than just hit the ball. We want someone to *see the great shot*. We want to improve as we go forward. We want to defeat an opponent. And you can bet we want to talk about it later in the clubhouse. Golf played in solitude has its occasional rewards and gives us the opportunity to work on aspects of our game, but the rewards never compare to the recognized performance. It's why we keep score and frame scorecards. Its why there are trophies and dinners following the tournaments we enter.

The emotional payoff in retirement has got to be

examined carefully and thoughtfully. It's not enough to say 'I don't have to work anymore,' or 'Now I've got some time on my hands.' There must be a plan that satisfies the emotions and the ego. Why do you think the S.C.O.R.E. program (Successful Core of Retired Executives) has such great participation?

Words like fulfillment and meaning, as squishy as they are, need to be considered or you run the risk of being disconnected.

NUMBER TWO: SPOUSAL CONSENT

"Give me golf clubs, fresh air and a beautiful partner, and you cankeep the clubs and the fresh air."
- Jack Benny

This is so often overlooked that it becomes one the greatest marital difficulties of the retired. When the notion of what retirement should look like is not a coordinated effort it can become a real drag. Everyone has heard the comments from the spouse who arrives on the home scene after decades of spending five days a week elsewhere, only to hear 'He's driving me crazy.' Of course this goes both ways. For all of recorded history men and women have been driving each other nuts, this is not news. But now with this event called retirement which is supposed to be a joyous occasion, comes the implication that it *really should be.* A lot of people put a smile on and speak lovingly about their new found freedom, only to sit at home wondering how they got to this point.

If you've ever played two-person best ball, you know that an absence of strategy is only going to frustrate both players. Some play it like it's only their score that matters.

When one partner hits a shot into trouble, and the other doesn't play safe, they could both lose the match. It is an event that demands coordination. You must ask yourselves questions like 'What are we going to do on hole #5?' 'Will our approaches and styles compliment one another out there today, or do we have to make some serious adjustments?'

Q: Travel? Travel a little? Travel a lot? Near? Far? Months? Weeks? Days?

Q: Go out to eat? Weekly? Monthly? On a whim? Same restaurant? New place every time?

Get the picture? Most certainly the issues get more difficult.

Q: Put mother (in-law) into a nursing home facility? Who pays? Siblings involved? What about the inheritance we may have planned on?

Q: Sell the home we've been in for 35 years? Buy a condo? Buy 2 condos?

Discussion, not avoidance.

NUMBER THREE:

'Playing Through' Your Spouse

"She (Mickey Wright) had the finest golf swing I ever saw."
- Ben Hogan

Over the years it seemed that golf, at times, had become a four letter word to my wife. Yet, strangely, almost mysteriously she began to develop an interest in the game (I blame a par 3 in Pompano Beach), paying it lip service for some time with some friends of hers who golf. She 'threatened' to enter my world with couple's golf outings. The people she was conspiring with were nice enough people, but the thought of the obligation of playing regularly in a foursome, half of which you could only hope would break 140 in a speedy six hours was frightening. Sure, you say, 'it doesn't have to be a weekly event', but once you've peered into that parallel universe it's only a matter of time before the gravitational pull gets you and you can't find the exit doors.

My only hope of salvaging my little universe was to propose that Bob and I played ahead of her and Carol, or at least reserve the right to play through them, even if we were in the same foursome. I am very aware that you don't typically play through your own foursome, but trust me, she hadn't read the rule book.

By doing so, I assured her, she wouldn't feel rushed. I would be able to order ahead in the clubhouse, change my golf shoes, pull the car around, take a lesson, and write a novel.

My point, which is certain to get me in deep trouble, is that our rounds don't have to necessarily finish together. Our enjoyment levels may both be wonderful, as long as we don't irritate each other's pace of play.

It seems that it is becoming a less frequent occurrence for a couple to coordinate the timing of their joint retirements, making it a seamless transition. More often than not life's circumstances presents one spouse's opportunities at some earlier juncture than the other. The acceleration of one person's retirement shouldn't force the other's decision. In fact, there are greater opportunities for adjustment with one easing into retirement earlier than with simultaneous retirement. There may be the reversal of some household duties or a change in who handles the social calendar. These always present challenges, but also lead to a greater appreciation of each others role. They may serve as a probationary period for experiencing the possibility of a partial social vacuum, and the stepped-down financial change in income without feeling the full brunt all at once. Gaps in medical coverage can be filled with this approach. Some of the most critical changes are the clock and calendar adjustments. Filling newly found chunks of time with meaningful activity can be a trial and error experiment which takes time. The important thing is to avoid 'when worlds collide.' Eventually, you'll both get to the club house.

NUMBER FOUR:

Absence makes the heart grow fonder...

Frustration is one of the greatest catalysts to initiating retirement. Getting out of the rat-race. Stopping the incessant traveling. Dealing with the bureaucracy. Co-workers who drive you crazy. Once you've unplugged from all of that, in the absence of something consistent and enjoyable, you may find that those people weren't as bad as they seemed. You know, you might just miss them. It is odd how sometimes the least likely candidate to return to the work place to visit, is the guy who said he'd never look back. He'll show up with donuts or bagels and grab your ear, or any ear, either because he has nothing else to do or because he's demonstrating his freedom to waste time without the consequence of termination.

You know why he's there of course. He misses you. He misses all the people, well *almost* all the people he used to complain about at home over the dinner table. He misses them because they were his network. They occupied most of his waking hours for at least five days a week. The adjustment in retirement requires a replacement of that network. As the old saying goes, nature abhors a vacuum. We all serve a purpose to the people we associate with even if they don't particularly care for us.

I know a man who, fairly abruptly, decided within one

year of retirement he was selling the house and moving south about 1000 miles. He had lived in his town all of his life, worked in that town all of his life, and had golfed with the same foursome for well over 30 years twice a week in season. Suffice to say, just because the golfing season got longer the further south he went, doesn't mean it was as enjoyable. The idiosyncrasies of his old foursome were predictable. He knew who he was going to take money from and who he was going to pay. He knew how to get in their head with a pull of the Velcro or a step across a line. The point is he went in cold and his regrets were significant. He lacked the network. He could have taken some time to develop it over a few years before he made the move, but the move was impulsive and not well thought out. He's driving his wife nuts.

NUMBER FIVE:

Too Expensive to play poorly, Too expensive to not enjoy:

If you've ever played a very expensive course you know the dilemma of which I speak. Imagine you have an opportunity to play Pebble Beach. Your possible once-in-a-lifetime opportunity gets you thinking...'I better play my best game today or I've wasted a lot of cash.' Then again, you begin to think...'Even if I don't play well, I'm going to soak up every minute of this experience'. So you commit to pay attention to every hole and its beautiful surrounding vista. You capture certain holes on camera, trying to get your money's worth from both quality and enjoyment. The question is, are they mutually exclusive? I've tried to do both and quite candidly, I couldn't. Every time I tried to stop and soak up the scenery it took my head out of my game and I miss hit more than my share. So I determined that those rare experiences were ones during which I was going to ignore the scorecard, and just take pleasure in the knowledge that I was on a golf course and that it was phenomenal. I would remember only the isolated good shot, not the total. Sometimes I would even toss the scorecard altogether.

The point here is that I had to boil it down and accept two things. First, I could afford to play. And second, I was going to plan my enjoyment.

After perhaps decades of building the habit of saving and sacrificing there is a degree of difficulty in making the transition to spending. We participate a long time in the accumulation phase of life only to feel as though we're required to enter the distribution phase almost overnight. The fear of lack enters the mind and can seriously impair the enjoyment of a stage of life you've looked forward to for a long time. There has to be a degree of knowing that you have enough to keep you from resenting every spent dollar. It would be better to continue to work than to enter a period of resentment.

Sometimes with couples the resentment is often directed at a spouse with startling reciprocity.

'I've worked too hard to be bled dry,' he says...

'I've worked too hard to be denied enjoyment,' she replies.

One thinks the other's spending habits need to be controlled. One blames the other for being too cheap. They are both often correct, and instead of finding a balanced approach they can agree upon which reduces stress, each continues to think he or she is the thermostat that must set the pace, and compensate for the other. Instead of moving towards one another to provide some balance they go in the opposite direction. Inevitably it results in overcompensation.

Knowing is the key. Guessing is the enemy. It is better to run the numbers, or have someone run them for you, to find out approximately how long your money will last or what the target number should be. Fear is very real and can rob you of the goal you've had for yourself.

Plan your enjoyment.

"As the retirement age pushes farther back and the finances for that time of life are less and less certain, it was almost unconscionable to not take advantage of the opportunity to travel now when I had the money and the health." Jesse Keller, age 32, quoted in the NY Times (6-8-06). He is young but he gets it. If you haven't done what he is doing, you owe it to yourself to set your plan in motion.

FEAR &
CLENCHING:
COUCH TIME

*"That little ball won't move until you hit it, and
there's nothing you can do for it after it has gone."*
-   Babe Didrikson Zaharias

I think Babe said it well. The anticipation that there
is no control over our shot after it is hit causes a
great deal of anxiety for golfers. It is the reason so
many thoughts go streaking through our heads before,
during and after our swing. Precious little time is spent
in actual contact between the ball and club. That
brevity and irreversibility leads to too many pre-shot
thoughts, most of which flood the mind as we stand
over the ball and during the back swing. At times we
would like to be Cyrano de Bergerac hiding in the
shadows, pining after what we desire so much, afraid
that our most hideous feature is about to make itself

known.

Of course thoughts can be of both the good and bad variety. It seems that their favorite time to appear is as we step to the ball to swing. The best thoughts of course are of the positive commitment sort. "I picked the right club" and "the yardage is correct" and best of all "I'm good with this club."

Good thoughts themselves don't increase our skill, but they do something almost as important. They keep us from being a big screw-up. How often have you had horribly negative thoughts over a shot only to see the self fulfilling prophecy of your worst imagination come to fruition? 'I'm gonna shank this…I always do with this club.'…SHANK! You can almost see it before it happens. Of course, slightly more seldom experienced is the good positive thought, followed by the good positive outcome.

I won't go much farther with this diatribe, because if you are the type that berates him or herself out on the course with bad thoughts, you probably deserve your outcome. Until you change your thought process, you'll get the same results. Lest I continue and be tempted to bill you for unlicensed psychotherapy, let's look at the impact this has in the investment world.

Thoughts won't cause your investments to perform better, but they can keep you from making the mistakes that cost money. Indecision, last minute anxiety, altering of well thought out plans, fear of volatility, over estimation of risk, etc. can all lead us to the shank.

Positive attitudes about well thought out investments, diversified portfolios with well understood risk and reward levels can only help to enhance your possibilities of success. Good committed thoughts will keep you from being erratic and undisciplined, keep you from abandoning an investment in the poorest of conditions when loss is certain. Just as with the golf shot there is a time for thought and a time for action. Once you reasonably assess what it is you are going to do and why you want to do it, then do it. Don't let a new set of thoughts invade your action.

"Half this game is ninety percent mental"
- Danny Ozark, Phillies' manager
(different game, great quote)

FAIRYTALES & OMISSIONS

"I don't exaggerate, I remember big."
-Chi Chi Rodriguez

"Isn't it fun to go out on the course and lie in the sun?"
- Bob Hope

Golf shares something in common with fishing. Fishing shares something in common with investing. They all have their tall tales. They all have their stories of the almost. In the words of agent Maxwell Smart... 'Missed it by *that* much.'

It may be the indoor lack of fresh air, or the adrenaline letdown of a final putt that causes it, but the grille rooms of America's golf courses are the amnesia epicenters of the universe. There is more lost in translation between reality and fantasy there than in a United Nations corruption investigation. You undoubtedly know of which I speak. It is not always everyone present, but a few usually have the new revisionist version of the round that was.

Just as exaggerations of grand proportions take place, omissions are not far behind. At times the stories are entertaining. When they become misleading we have crossed the line. Especially when the misleading give some the inclination that you should follow suit, as in the world of investing. Errors or omissions of fact if taken seriously can lead some people to put a great deal of their own capital at risk. Someone's puffing up of themselves can lead others to make bad decisions. The actions are often taken spontaneously and without much research...wouldn't want to miss out on something great by waiting a couple of weeks, now would we?

A guy I know bought very expensive woods because on the range where he tested them they hit so well. When he brought them out to the course he couldn't get them to stay anywhere close to the fairway. If you had listened to him sing the praises of these clubs the day he bought them you would have been tempted to run out and buy a set. If you had waited two weeks and been walking in the woods along the course, he would have given you a cerebral contusion.

A gentleman I dealt with made a similar but far more serious financial mistake. Just days before he implemented his plan, he took one third of his entire portfolio and invested it in one stock. This was a figure comfortably in the six figures. He had had his daughter's future in-laws up for the week end and they began to discuss stocks and his interest was piqued. Two days later he bought the stock at about $52 a share. It briefly went up to $60 a share and shortly thereafter cascaded to $5 a share. However, once they settled the class action law suit for misrepresenting sales numbers, the value went straight to zero. They are still his daughter's in-laws, but they don't visit too much anymore.

Knowing how things fit your particular circumstances, and how they will perform under pressure, is what counts. Everything starts off shiny and clean, not everything finishes that way.

PROCRASTINATION & PERFECTIONISM

"No one will ever have golf under his thumb. No round will ever be so good it could not have been better. Perhaps this is why golf is the greatest of all games. You are not playing a human adversary; you are playing a game. You are playing old man par."
- Bobby Jones

These twins have had some effect on all of us. It seems that they always go hand in hand.

"I'll take a look at our statements *next month*."

"Let's wait until *after the first of the year* to review the portfolio."

Procrastination is a derivative of perfectionism. We know that when we actually sit down and analyze what we've done, it won't be perfect. It will come up comparatively short in some way to something else out there. We will find the gap between last year's amazing stock performer and our portfolio, and it's likely to be bigger than we could imagine.

But there is always a gap. There is always something better. How we deal with the fact that we didn't participate in it is the bigger issue.

One of the differences between great golfers and average golfers is what they see in their mind's eye.

The good ones always imagine that the shot they will hit will come off exactly as they imagined it. Does it? Of course not. Sometimes it's close and sometimes it's not. But if they hit a horrible shot they don't start imagining every shot afterwards being horrible. Their imagination doesn't begin to produce pictures of golf ugliness. They have learned the discipline of striving to be consistent both in thought and action.

So it should be with our financial progress. Just because we've taken some lumps doesn't mean all future attempts will be as unsuccessful. If we begin to pay attention to the gap between perfection and performance we will invite procrastination.

Has anyone ever procrastinated their way to success? As Jim Rohn has said, 'You always pay the price. It is either the price of discipline or the price of regret. Discipline weighs ounces, regret weighs tons.'

"You don't understand! I coulda had class. I coulda been a contender. I could've been somebody, instead of a bum, which is what I am." - Marlon Brando, **On the Waterfront,** *1954*

EMOTIONS : FEAR & GREED

"No passion so effectually robs the mind of all its
powers of acting and reasoning as fear."
- Edmund Burke

The USGA has numerous formulas for assessing the difficulty of a course. What they call the Obstacle Stroke Value is a numerical evaluation comprising various hazards and trouble. Topography, the size of the greens, the width of the fairway in landing areas, trees, water, etc. are all part of the equation. The last component, what they call the Psychology factor is 'a measurement of the cumulative effect of the other nine obstacles.' So it is not just you having internal torment. The professionals at the USGA stand behind the notion that you should occasionally snap out there. Go ahead and lose it, it's already part of the equation. Just don't let it sap your confidence.

One of the most intriguing statistics that the PGA Tour keeps is what they call 'Bounce Back.' It measures a player's ability to score well after a bad hole. What qualifies as a bounce back is a birdie or better, immediately following a score of bogey or worse on the previous hole.

In his record setting season of 2004 Vijay Singh was number four in bounce back. Guess who was number one...John Daly. He was voted "Comeback Player of the Year." In Tiger's record setting year of 2000 he was ranked number one in bounce back. It is a great measurement of confidence.

Fear and lack of confidence can kill or disable a career. The name David Duval comes to mind, although he still may have a comeback.

Just ask Ian Baker-Finch, "When you lose that trust and you lose that belief...you start second guessing...The more pressure, the more tension, the higher the score." *(Baker-Finch in GOLF DIGEST Jan '05)*
The year after his stunning 1991 British Open victory he fell to 151st on the bounce back list. Eventually, he traded his putter for a microphone.

'I will not be denied.' That is the message of confidence. It holds true for your financial future as well. 'Oh, gimme a break' you may say, 'the performance of investments is so far out of my grasp, my confidence has nothing to do with it.'

Don't we measure collective confidence with the Consumer Confidence Index to try to gauge how much people will buy this holiday season? How would you measure your individual financial confidence?

Individually, haven't you ever been tempted to pull out of the market because it seems to just keep going down? I've seen clients do it despite advice to the contrary. They inevitably miss the upturn and get back in much too late, if at all.

Did you ever experience a 'pop up?' I don't mean the pop up camper, I'm talking about the pop up thought. The type that pops up when you're over a shot and gives you mixed messages.

'I don't know if I can make this...'
'Don't swing from the outside...'
'Don't slice it here...'

These thoughts are along the same lines as the thoughts that come when you're investing and you've got a decision to make. In golf, our mind, body and emotions are connected. When investing, the mind, emotions and checkbook are connected. Impulsiveness comes on both the buy and sell side of the equation. Trends or patterns seem to convince us that action is imperative. Here are the primary two thoughts that cause investment error:

'It's been going up, don't miss out...'
- causes you to buy high.

'It's been going down, get out before its too late...'
- causes you to sell low.

Scientists tell us that we put too much trust in trends. As we see a pattern develop we become convinced of its legitimacy. We even produce chemicals in the brain that lend themselves to a higher level of trust. They have developed an entire branch of research called neuroeconomics to study the phenomenon that occurs in our minds involving money and decision making. To put it succinctly, we don't deal emotionally well with delayed gratification. Our prefrontal cortex needs to be well developed and in good functioning condition. We produce oxytocin which is connected to our ability to develop trust. See, I knew I should have paid more attention in anatomy class.

Your confidence should be in the plan. Your plan. The bigger picture it paints takes your focus off of one bad stock, one bad quarter or one bad year. It should be clear enough and well thought out enough to anticipate bad news. Good advisors have always told their clients that if you want the returns of the stock market you need to be able to handle a 25-30% drop some years. You should have a strategy to stick to when hard times come in the economy, or in your personal circumstances.

In golf, a plan helps us step to the ball with a desired outcome, and lets us trust our swing. Once you've done your best to stick to the plan you can mentally 'let go' of the results – good shot or bad shot, market up or market down.

Strategy took Phil Mickelson from zero-for-46 in majors to a Masters win the spring after the worst year in his professional career. On the 72nd tee he knew a 3 wood gave him a better chance at birdie than an errant driver. He has since won more majors. That was Mickelson with a plan, versus Mickelson with a wish. Which was unfortunately followed by Mickelson with two drivers at the 'I'm such an idiot' Open.

A herd mentality is not a plan. Following your

neighbor's decisions is not a plan. Your plan is your road map, your guide during upside and downside. It not only keeps you on track with measurable expectations, but it should keep out the worries and sleepless nights It's all about achieving emotional equilibrium.

BEAR MARKETS AND HOSEL SHOTS

"Golf is a game in which you try to put a small ball in a small hole with implements singularly unsuited to the purpose."
- Winston Churchill

Money and golf, golf and money. They both have that mercurial quality about them. Just as you think you have mastered one, it can evaporate before your eyes. Attaching too much emotion to either can be the downfall of both. How many times has someone quit the game of golf, thrown clubs, or made an oath never to come back to the course?

Here's the pattern. You are introduced to golf. You begin to take an interest in it. You experience a period of improved skills and develop an almost cocky attitude toward the game. You see an ever-increasing incline of improvement in your future, shaving shots off of your total. You begin to read virtually everything ever written about the game and become a student of golf minutiae. Then out of nowhere, on a day of perfect sunshine and ideal temperatures, it sneaks up on you. The sh...., the shaa...., the shanggg...., let's just call it the 'lateral hosel shot.'

When the game first gets away from you, you lie awake in bed wondering if you've experienced a curse. In your dreams you see someone sticking needles into a little doll during it's backswing, and the doll bears a striking resemblance to you. It is your slump. You ponder the possibility of whether it will ever come back.

It is an experience equaled only by your first 'bear market.' You haven't experienced a set back of any significance before in your brief engagement and now, just as you feel fully committed, it turns on you. You are not alone. Invest long enough and you will be caught by one. The warning signs include straight line projections of accumulation. Comments like, "at this rate of growth I will have over a million by...."

How often have you noticed that the personalities that seem to best handle either investing or golf are those who can keep the emotions in check? The personalities who can detach themselves from the results and give great attention to the facts and circumstances alone, seem to be the ones who make progress. That is not to say that emotions are totally uninvolved, not at all. But the invitation to be emotional in either endeavor is usually counterproductive. Most golfers who have quit playing the game cite one or more of the following reasons:

- it takes too much time
- it's too expensive
- takes too long to learn
- is too difficult

The same could be said for retirement investing.

Leaving doesn't solve anything and never lends itself to mastery.

PSYCHOBABBLE

"Success in this game depends less on strength of
body than strength of mind..."
- Arnold Palmer

Dysfunctions, episodes, disturbances, aversions, phobias...they are all excuses in the world of golf. Our current society is one bent on legitimizing poor behavior. It's always someone else's fault, and when that fails, here's my clinical excuse. In order to be as politically incorrect as possible I have listed here (a few) and in the appendix, as many issues as I could think of that might be used to explain your golfing buddies' behavior, and some might even translate well to the financial realm.

Antisocial personality disorder: pervasive pattern of disregard for and violation of the rights of others, failure to conform to social norms, deceitfulness, impulsivity, irritability, unwillingness to meet financial obligations. Sound like anybody in your foursome?

Developmental coordination disorder: performance in daily activities that require motor coordination is substantially below that expected given the person's chronological age and measured intelligence.

Dissociative trance disorder: single or episodic disturbances in the state of consciousness or memory which are indigenous to particular locations, i.e. golf courses especially in the vicinity of a scorecard.

Agoraphobia: Anxiety about being in places or situations from which escape might be difficult or embarrassing, or in which help may not be available in the event of having an unexpected panic attack. Often occurring on bridges, in crowds, sand traps, or deep rough.

It is fairly apparent that your round or entire golfing lifetime could become one long string of episodic dysfunctions resulting in you looking like some twisted piece of mental origami. If you haven't been the perpetrator, then some of this has undoubtedly slipped into the lives of some of your playing partners.

The psychological component of the game of golf is both deceptive and delightful. It will allow for you to singularly celebrate one memorable shot to the point that it is all you require to return some day for another round. On the other hand, it is capable of burdening you with enough mental overhead that the internal discussion you have over every shot sounds much like a sinister version of Handel's hallelujah chorus.

The psychological connection to financial decisions can be equally debilitating or rewarding.

Remember, to be used correctly, it always 'them'. It's *never* you.

VISUALIZATION:

"Go confidently in the direction of your dreams! Live the life you've imagined. As you simplify your life, the laws of the universe will be simpler."
– Henry David Thoreau

Every golf coach will tell you how important it is to visualize your shot ahead of time. Picture the shot. Imagine the ball's flight. See it landing on the spot you aimed for. If you've tried this consistently, you know it can improve your game. As you've heard, the human brain will act based on what you tell it or show it. It can't tell the difference between a bad image or a good one. Visualizing a shot gives your brain a message it can identify with and respond to.

So let me ask you to take this brief survey: What will your 'retirement' look like? Will it...

- involve a career change?
- involve part-time work?
- involve re-education?
- involve volunteer time?
- involve golf from sunrise to sunset?

Your picture of that lifestyle will dramatically affect its outcome. It is not likely you will stumble upon a second career or a master's degree without the planning. Taking time to determine what you would like to happen, what you would like to be involved in, is your shot visualization. It will keep your talents, skills and knowledge from being diffused. It needs to be specific, as detailed as possible and preferably in writing. It will evolve over time and needs to remain flexible.

Regularly repeating that exercise will keep you focused. It will become a pre-shot routine of sorts. It will also serve as a filter to other intruding thoughts, the type that can be distracting or debilitating.

IRRATIONAL EXUBERANCE

*"Concentration comes out of a combination of
confidence and hunger. "
- Arnold Palmer*

Have you noticed how a bad attitude in a foursome can spread like a virus? It can be intrusive enough to cause all four members to miss-hit shots. A contagiously positive attitude can also lift the countenance of a group. It can relieve stress and bring the best out in everyone.

In this era of media influence and quick delivery of information, collective panic leads to widespread downturns, just as collective elation leads to 'irrational exuberance' (thank you Mr. Greenspan).

On the individual front the same imaginations can bring similar personal results. It happens in many formats but usually begins with a narrowing of one's vision by any number of reasons. Familiarity is one culprit. Often someone presumes that their familiarity with an industry, a stock, or a market gives them a false sense of security. Have you ever known anyone who convinced himself that growth in a particular area (stock, real estate, pharmaceutical development) would be a never ending incline? They overweight themselves to the exclusion of other assets. End result? Timing is rarely perfect.

The same is true on the downside. A sector once burned will '*never recover.*' A market once depressed '*won't come back.*' That fatalistic mindset causes many people to miss the opportunities. It prevents any sort of contrarian confidence. The 'I will not be denied' opportunity.

Have you ever noticed how Tiger Woods, of all the top ten players on the PGA Tour money list, often spends the least amount of time in the fairway. He is however, among the top few in Greens in Regulation. The shots that would otherwise kill most other players are seen as challenges by Tiger. His recovery abilities are significant, and more importantly he sees the challenge as an opportunity. His success with those shots is part skill, (and as most golfers know to be very true) a large part attitude. His attitude lends confidence to how he views the shot, how he selects from the various possibilities and finally, how he executes the shot.

PLAYING YOUR ROUND

"The best way to win by one stroke is to try to win by two."
– Gary Player

THE FRONT NINE

"You can talk about strategy all you want, but what really matters is resiliency."
- Hale Irwin

W e initially discussed that as you point toward retirement, the start of your round often begins without you knowing it. It starts with your first job, your first opportunity to put some real long term money away no matter how small. It is that 'smallness' that is the culprit. Meager contributions early don't look like they will add much to your accumulations later, but they will. In fact, they do more than just add to your nest egg. They set the stage for your discipline of investing, your attitude toward market volatility, your hope for recovery, and your appreciation for the balance between risk and reward.

Think about a round of golf that begins with four or five pretty good holes. Pars, maybe a couple of bogeys, no disasters, no implosions early. What does that do for you? It gives you hope for a round that could still be special. It lets you stay within yourself and not feel desperate to perform better than usual on an ever decreasing number of holes.

Conversely, how do you feel when you are well over par after just four or five holes. Throw some snowmen on the card early and now you're just biding time or possibly pulling your driver out for everything hoping to make up lost ground.

The front nine is about pace, it's about gradually building momentum and getting yourself to a point where one bad shot does not put you into a state of desperation. It is about smart recovery shots and managed risk. In the golf round you do not get to consult with your coach as you play, however, in the financial round you do. You have the opportunity to get another opinion, make subtle changes and find your rhythm again. You are able to put away the club that won't cooperate or make an adjustment in strategy up ahead.

Not many courses employ them any more, but caddies

are permitted to go with you. You may think of them in the context of coach, advisor or sounding board if you wish, but ideally they have walked that course before with enough other people and have enough experience to know some of what lies ahead. Use them to avoid hazards mostly.

The financial front nine is characterized by periodic investments. It is the start of your accumulation phase and it comes in installments. It may encompass your entire working career, but it has a good degree of marginal utility attached to it. By that, I mean that the earlier the contributions made, the more impact they have. The later they come the less opportunity they have for compounding. That is not to say that you shouldn't contribute in your late fifties or early sixties. Those are the deposits that will fund the furthest years of your back nine. When you are in your 80's you'll be glad you invested when you were in your 60's.

MAKING THE TURN

*"Golf is a game in which you claim the privileges of
age and retain the playthings of childhood."*
-Samuel Johnson

It is the brief moment in your round when you often pause to assess where you are on your score card, catch your breath, grab a burger and try to formulate some strategy for what's ahead. Of course, that strategy is often dictated by what has transpired up to this point. On the course this often involves about all of five minutes and the interruption of finding the ketchup and mustard. In the financial arena it should incorporate more time, more questions, and fewer condiments. On the course you get enough time to grab the burger, but not to consult anyone on what they've seen in your game. In your finances, you need to consult.

In the arena of retirement it literally is the turn. It is a turning from a focus on accumulation to a greater emphasis and concern for distribution. Will I have enough to live on if I retired now? How much more will I need to make sure I have enough to feed my family going forward? It isn't necessarily the actual moment of stopping earned income and beginning to live off of your accumulated investments. It may be close to that moment in time, but it is more a thought moment. It is a shift or turn to the concern about generating a sustainable withdrawal from your retirement sources.

Just as the landscape of your golf course may be very different between the front and back, the considerations of your front nine and back nine should be assessed at the turn.

Your focus to this point has been accumulation. It has involved longer time horizons before the need to use your funds than you have now. You will soon need to use your funds to replace your earned income and that means that your risk tolerance should change. If you are on track with your accumulation, you no longer will be able to tolerate the same volatility as you may have in the past. Why? Because a portfolio hurt by wide swings in volatility has time to recover while you went about earning an income. Now a portfolio which takes a big drop not only has the reduction in capital to make up, but it is also likely to give up some of its capital to you as income flow. During retirement your withdrawals are fairly consistent, your returns are not. That can hurt long term more than you imagine.

Consider the following portfolio examples:

Portfolio	A	B	C
Yr. 1	-20%	35%	12%
2	-10	25	18
3	-5	30	17
4	30	20	14
5	25	15	-8
6	20	10	-18
7	30	5	30
8	10	-8	15
9	-5	-15	25
10	25	-17	-25
Average	10%	10%	8%

If you had invested $100,000 in each of these portfolios, and at the end of the first year began to pull out 6% for income (and increased that income by 3.5% for inflation) for 10 years, you would have very different ending balances. Even though **Portfolios A and B** averaged 10%, their sequence of returns were very different. The early losses in **A** caused it to have an ending balance of $88,862.

Portfolio B had the same average return, but its losses came later in the sequence, resulting in an ending balance of $161,203. Their compounded rates of return were very different from one another. **Portfolio C** which had an average return of only 8% had an ending balance of $105,747. How can it be that an average return of 8% beat one of 10%? Sequence of returns.

When you begin to take money from your accumulation, the volatility and sequence of returns becomes incredibly important. How can steady bogey golf beat erratic golf with pars, birdies and a hand full of blow-up holes? Because this isn't match play. Life is stroke play. *Bad holes count.*

If you have done poorly, you'll need some guidance on how to make reparations and jump start your plan. Even if you have done amazingly well, (and make sure you have actually done well, and aren't imagining that you're way ahead) you'll need to get some very important tax advice. More assets lead to larger issues, larger consequences, and the need for bigger solutions.

So, are you way behind? What kind of trouble did you encounter up to this point? What's working for you? What's not working for you? Have you paid attention to your financial business to this point or have you generally ignored it, just hoping for the best? Do you have a spectacular round going? Have you learned some positive lessons about economic cycles and opportunities?

"I know I'm getting better at golf because I'm hitting fewer spectators."
- President Gerald Ford

BACK NINE

"Competitiveness is a personality thing, and competitive people don't become pushovers the day they turn 50."
- Hale Irwin

This is your home stretch. This is the part of the game you hope to get in before dark. Most people would guess that the 18th hole is retirement and the clubhouse is the great retirement objective. Not so.

Now you begin a different type of juggling act which involves not only today but many tomorrows from now. Your game continues because you have to be both defensive with your shot selection and still look for some scoring opportunities. There will be no driving the par fours now. It's all about the short grass. You must walk the tight-rope of income today and growth in the future. There is no time or tolerance for out-of-bounds left or right. You need fairways and crisp irons.

If strategy was important up to this point it becomes irreplaceable now. There will be more anxiety as the specter of jeopardizing the lump gives way to some clenching. Now is the time for the pre-shot routine and an easy swing.

If you were to compare the strategy of the front nine to the back nine they would look a lot like the difference between Portfolio A and C in the previous section. You should be looking for pars, not birdies. If the birdies come that's great, but it will not involve going for the par five in two.

A few considerations are worth noting. You may be coming out of a corporate plan and need to roll over you 401k into your own IRA. Or you may need to find a way to convert a large number of stocks acquired over the years into something that will generate a cash flow. You may be one of the ever decreasing numbers that need to make a choice between a lump sum payout or a steady pension.

None of the answers are easy, nor can they be boiled down into 'one size fits all' templates. Some of the basics however, include keeping your costs relatively low, finding guarantees where applicable, and diversifying to an appropriate risk level. Ease of management should also be a factor unless you are inclined to run your own funds and have your own successful track record that involved both market upturns and especially downturns.

There are many strategies to shaping your income stream. These are a few:

- Make at least 25% of your income (aside from Social Security) of a fixed, non-variable nature. The balance of your assets should be diversified to your personal risk tolerance.
- Match your fixed income to your fixed expenses and your variable income to your

variable expenses. Mortgage, utilities, regular household expenses could be covered by the type of income from a fixed annuity or fixed pension. Your variable expenses, travel and entertainment for instance, can be taken from your assets that produce varying returns.

- Invest your assets according to when they will be used. Assets to be used soonest would be invested most conservatively, progressively later assets would be invested progressively more aggressively. The replenishing of the earliest dollars would come from essentially sliding the assets toward the more conservative every few years.

Wouldn't it be nice to play your round in the order and sequence of your choosing. Play the easiest holes first to see how far ahead you can get then leave the hard holes for later once you are warmed up and have some 'feel good' scores behind you.

Or perhaps you would like to get the tough ones out of the way first, take your lumps early and have the smooth sailing left. Unfortunately that is not the pattern the course architects gave us, nor is it the course the Great Architect gave us. We play them as they come. The best we can do is to be ready.

"Golf happens to be almost a perfect sport."
- Dr. Laurel Coleman, geriatrician,
"Golf for Women" Magazine January 2006

This past fall, I had the pleasure of meeting a gentleman on my home course. He and I played nine holes together and as I watched him play, I thought to myself 'this guy is pretty good for a senior citizen.' Reasonably long drives, always in the short grass, nice touch around the greens. I figured he was about 70 years old. Well, on the fifth hole he gave me the brief Jack McDonough story...He lives on a lake nearby, splits his time between New Hampshire and Florida, and he is a widower who just lost his wife of nearly 60 years. Sixty years! So much for my age assumption. He was eighty-five years old. What really shocked me was that he had taken up the sport when he was 71. It seemed as though he hadn't aged a day since he picked up a club. Always quick to amass creative excuses to play, I concluded that golf must be the environmental equivalent of the fountain of youth. Thinking it would carry the same weight as a doctor's note, I asked him to write a note to my wife about the wonders of golf and how it would preserve me. She didn't buy it. In fact, she said preservation was not exactly what she had in mind. At eighty-five years old and in great health he still had a lot to be thankful for. He did say he had his eye on a rich widow. It's always good to have a plan B.

CONCLUSION

*"The future, according to some scientists, will be
exactly like the past, only far more expensive."*
– John Sladek

Running out of money in retirement is like running out
of money on the fourth day of a seven day cruise.
Those last three days are no fun. So, in the face of so
many challenges, how will you fare? You must deal
with the internal challenge of thoughts and
expectations, the external hurdles and pressures of
poor demographics and the inevitable confiscatory
increase in taxes.

The future in my opinion is going to look like a U.S.
Open set up with high rough, slick greens and stiff
headwinds. But is will also be a time of great and
unique opportunities most of which we haven't seen
yet. If we do not familiarize ourselves with everything
in our bag, we will miss the opportunities. You must
get a handle on what is your par, and develop the
discipline to move towards it.

Early in our round we know what our aspirations are. Few begin with plans of something less than mediocrity. Yet there is more to the equation than the obvious distinctions of our preferred destinations in life. The journey to those places is what can give us or rob us of fulfillment. When you put the pencil to your scorecard, how we spend our life matters more than how we spend our money. Money itself has no inherent virtue. The purposes we attach to money make it useful or useless. Along the way in achieving our plan, we have the opportunities to help others. It is the rule of life that giving to others never seems to diminish what we have. The universal principal of sowing and reaping is at work in both the good and bad. It is so much more enjoyable to get ahead of the curve on the good side.

Of all the attempts to define success, the best definition I have heard is this:

Success is designing a plan for your life, and then pulling it off.

The details are left to you.

Golf to the golf lover is a subject of great passion. If others have not been introduced to the game, our enthusiasm can be sufficiently infectious to get them started. We tell our children about the virtues of the game and its life lessons. If that passion translated over to the issue of finances and the accountability that went with it, we would impart responsibility unto our society that could meet the needs of much of what ails the world.

Finishing well takes consistent commitment especially when things don't seem to be on track. Keep your fundamentals working, and don't bite for every slick promotion. Focus on your scoring clubs, pay attention to the short game and make sure you bring enough balls to finish. May your last shots bring the excitement you had hoped for early on, and may you impart a passion to others for them to get off to the right start and finish well. Then for all of us, it's off to the 19th hole, the great grille room of judgment. No faking it there.

"Ultimately the people who win, who achieve victory in life are the people who are committed to it. They outlast everybody else. Because quite frankly all success in business, all success in relationships, all success in life comes at the end of the road of commitment!"
- Chris Widener

"The purpose of life is not to be happy. It is to be useful, to be honorable, to be compassionate, to have it make some difference that you have lived and lived well."
- Ralph Waldo Emerson

DELETED SCENES

The following chapters never made it past the editing room floor:

- Proper Alignment for Your Fourth Putt

- How to Hit a Titleist from the Rough When You Hit a Callaway from the Tee

- How to Avoid the Water When You Lie 8 in a Bunker

- How to Get More Carry from a Shank

- How to Develop a Smoker's Cough to Increase Earnings

- How to Sneak a 6 Hour Round onto the 'Honey-Do' List.

- How to Find That Ball That Everyone Else Saw Go in the Water

- Why Your Spouse Doesn't Care about Your Score.

- Using Visualization Techniques When Hitting Five Off the Tee

- Timely Use of Swing Suggestions for Your Opponent

- Using a Vardon Grip on Your Ball Retriever

- Purchasing the Proper Shoe for the Most Effective Foot Wedge.

- A 52 year old golfer gives a 19 year old cart girl $10 for a five dollar beer. Who has the higher IQ?

14 clubs – the official limit of clubs you may carry during competitive play. In money, it's the concept of diversification that reminds you to have more than a few tools in your bag, because different circumstances require different approaches.

EatWell/Sleep Well – the balance you must strike between risk and sacrifice now and comfort later. Incur too much risk now and your sleep quotient hits the skids. Play it too safe now and you'll have an eat-well problem in the future (as in macaroni and bologna for dinner.)

Executive Course – a circumstance where you've got a very short time frame to accomplish a round. Par looks enticing on this short course, but risk is something you can't afford now. Better leave the driver at home.

Annulment - the marriage mulligan.

Compounding – earnings from earnings, or conversely debt upon debt as in the case of credit cards left unpaid. **Golf equivalent**: hacking away in a bunker adding stroke upon stroke because of a bad shot in the first place. Get out safely and take your medicine. Take a drop.

Breakfast Ball – a first tee shot mulligan/excuse for the early morning tee time when you're not quite warmed up yet. May also be used after lunch depending upon age and flexibility. Forget about it, you're hitting three off the tee.

Depression – sever economic downturn characterized by high unemployment, falling prices, etc. **Golf equivalent**: state of mind experienced when your game goes from bad to worse, marked by continuous disbelief in your pathetic circumstances and a dastardly smirk on the face of your playing partner(s).

Yield – annual return on an investment. **Golf equivalent**: How much you regularly extort from your playing victims, or how much they can count on from you…regularly.

Margin Account – buying securities with borrowed funds (good if they go up, bad if they go down). **Golf equivalent**: paying shipping and handling for the free trial of a club and returning it if you don't like it, but paying full price if you damage it…even if you hate it.

Equitable Stroke Control = Alternative Minimum Tax (limits posting high scores to affect your handicap, AMT limits the deductibility of deductions to reduce your taxes.)

Alternative Minimum Tax – a tax law provision that has a different formula if your taxes end up too low to Uncle Sam's liking on your initial normal calculation. **Golf Equivalent**: a screwball scoring system that the scam artist in your foursome uses in the clubhouse to cause you to part with your cash and buy the beverages. Generally easy to spot because of the accompanying fast talking.

BIPSIC – Ball in pocket, sitting in cart. Things have

gotten so unbearable that for the good of the foursome and for the good of the game you've picked up your ball, waived your white flag and surrendered (conceded) the hole. **Financial Equivalent**: BIPSIC's are very personal as financial disasters go and are seldom discussed at cocktail parties or in steam rooms. A temporary attitude of 'hey, the score isn't important, I'm working on certain parts of my game' might mask your embarrassment until you get to the next tee box.

Churning - excessive trading done in a person's brokerage account in order to generate commissions (a very illegal activity). **Golf equivalent**: the revolving door of demo clubs, constantly buying, selling and trading clubs and barely finishing a round with the same set of clubs in order to find the elusive 'perfect' combination. Unfortunately, this activity is not illegal.

Closed end fund – a mutual fund that issues a fixed number of shares. Once sold, no new purchases are available. Shares may be purchased from existing shareholders. **Golf equivalent**: the limited membership private golf club, where the waiting line is full of those rooting for death or bankruptcy of at least a few of those on the inside.

European Union – an intergovernmental organization of 15 European countries. Currency, the Euro, presenting itself as a formidable rival to the U.S. dollar in worldwide exchanges. **Golf equivalent**: European Ryder Cup team, exhibiting great team play capable of spanking an uptight U.S. team.

U. S. House of Representatives – Branch of government charged with the responsibility of introducing spending bills and tax legislation. **Golf equivalent**: USGA (United States Golf Association) makes the rules (rules officials = IRS agents, complete with penalty assessments, only friendlier.)

Turnover – excessive selling of positions in your portfolio which can cause higher tax liabilities and unfavorable tax brackets. **Golf equivalent**: your trailing hand prematurely turns over your front hand usually producing a horribly errant shot.

Volatility – the measure of fluctuation from a mean, usually measured expressed by 'standard deviation'. Think 'big scary' roller coaster versus the 'itty bitty' kiddie coaster. **Golf equivalent**: How far away to the left or the right your shot goes from where you were aiming. How far often determines how good your recovery shot must be. (Also refers to your temper after an errant shot and whether you finish with the same number of clubs you started with.)

Double Miss – the condition of uncontrollably missing shots both to the left and to the right. As Tiger has said, "You can't aim a double miss." Meaning you can't aim one way to offset a shot that could end up going either way.

Pre Shot Routine – the predictable and reliable steps taken before each shot to remove anxiety and help produce a smooth flowing swing. **Financial equivalent**: doing a regular fundamental analysis of an investment before buying or selling used specifically to take the emotion out of the process. Rebalancing to an allocation mix is a form of pre-shot routine, if it's done automatically.

Pro Shop – the marketplace. It's full of lots of stuff, most of it shiny and attractive, but sadly the majority is unnecessary and a lot of it is overkill. **Financial equivalent**: get your bag of tools, make them quality and work them until they need to be replaced.

Trajectile Dysfunction - going off in the wrong direction. Some of those with this ailment continue for years without ever confronting the issue. Some of their closest friends are uncomfortable giving advice or counsel regarding the issue. Occasionally, someone with a worse case presents himself as an expert, only to be mocked and snickered at behind his back.

Fringe – that place just off of the putting surface, no sense measuring because you're not winning closest to the pin. Close but no cigar.

False Front- the visual technique used by architects to give you the impression that the green starts closer than it actually does, causing you to take less club than necessary. Like the low cost trading houses that would have you think you are going to save a ton of cash and accumulate much more by doing it yourself. Do the math, but I warn you it'll take a few years to figure out.

Two Person Scramble-The husband/wife tag team retirement accumulation plan. Over the course of their working lives they compare the retirement plans they each have alternately convinced that one or the other is superior. The one in the best position to take advantage of a great plan should be maxing out their contribution, no questions.

GLOSSARY: FEAR OF

Long Waits – Macrophobia

Voices or Noises, speaking aloud or telephones- Phonophobia.

Thunder and lightning- Astraphobia, Astrapophobia, Brontophobia or Keraunophobia – healthy fear…just ask Lee Trevino or Retief Goosen.

Thunder- Ceraunophobia

Thinking- Phronemophobia

Technology- Technophobia…resulting in 1972 irons, and woods actually made from trees.

Self, being alone- Autophobia, Eremophobia, Eremiphobia or Isolophobia.

Storm, thunder- Brontophobia.

Steep slopes- Bathmophobia

Snow- Chionophobia along w/ fear of number 8 = Fear of the scorecard snowman (Octo-chionophobia?)

Rain- Ombrophobia or Pluviophobia

Walking- Ambulophobia, Basistasiphobia or Basostasophobia.

Water- Hydrophobia

School - going to school, being 'taken to school'- Didaskaleinophobia

Narrow places or things - Stenophobia.

Pins- Enetophobia

Parents-in-law- Soceraphobia - thrown in just because it's a good one.

Mother-in-law- Pentheraphobia. Ditto

Old, growing- Gerascophobia or Gerontophobia

Number 8- Octophobia

Number 13- Triskaidekaphobia, always popular

Noises, loud- Ligyrophobia

Money- Chrometophobia or Chrematophobia

Marriage- Gamophobia- just because you probably know someone…

Left-handed; objects at the left side of the body- Sinistrophobia

Lakes- Limnophobia

Knowledge- Gnosiophobia or Epistemophobia

Insanity- Dementophobia or Maniaphobia – just because it presents an interesting catch 22

Flying- Aviophobia or Aviatophobia – will kill a good golf road trip

Forests or wooden objects- Xylophobia

Dependence on others- Soteriophobia – a good motivation to plan your retirement well.

Defeat- Kakorrhaphiophobia

Dawn or daylight- early tee times – Eosophobia

Crowded public places like markets, municipal courses on weekends- Agoraphobia

Car or vehicle, riding in- Amaxophobia – another killer of golf road trips

Bogeyman or bogies- Bogyphobia – honest, it really is.

Body, things to the left side of the body- Levophobia.

Body, things to the right side of the body-Dextrophobia.

Everything- Panophobia, Panphobia, Pamphobia, or Pantophobia

"Golf isn't a game, it's a choice that one makes with one's life."
– Charles Rosin, Northern Exposure

Printed in the United States
200458BV00001B/1-51/A